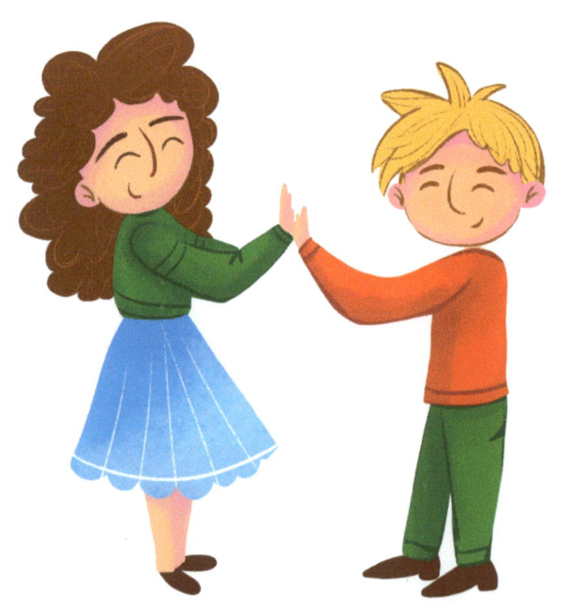

The Hourglass of Life

Written By
Mona Liza Santos

Illustrated By
Elena Sosnina

The Hourglass of Life
A Whirl of Fun and Wisdom for Young Minds!

Published by World Love Press

To request permissions, please contact:

missmonaliza81@yahoo.com

ISBN: 978-1-955560-34-4 (Paperback)
ISBN: 978-1-959805-09-0 (Hardcover)
ISBN: 978-1-959805-11-3 (E-book)
ISBN: 978-1-959805-10-6 (Audiobook)

Library of Congress Control Number: 2023903260

Illustrations by Elena Sosnina

First printing edition 2023.

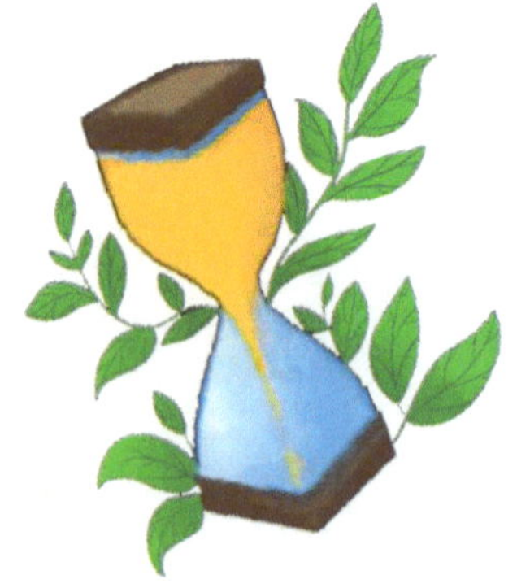

www.monalizasantos.com

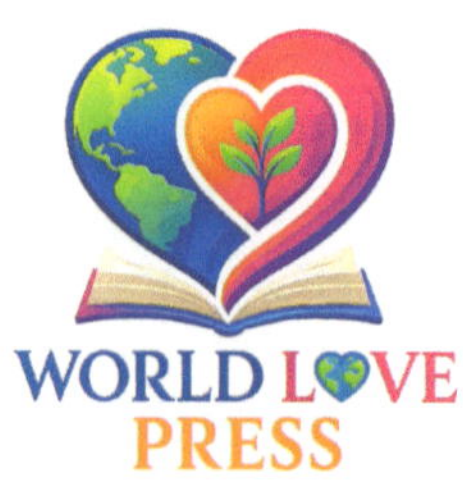

"Our lives are but specks of dust falling through the fingers of time. Like sands of the hourglass, so are the days of our lives."

—Socrates

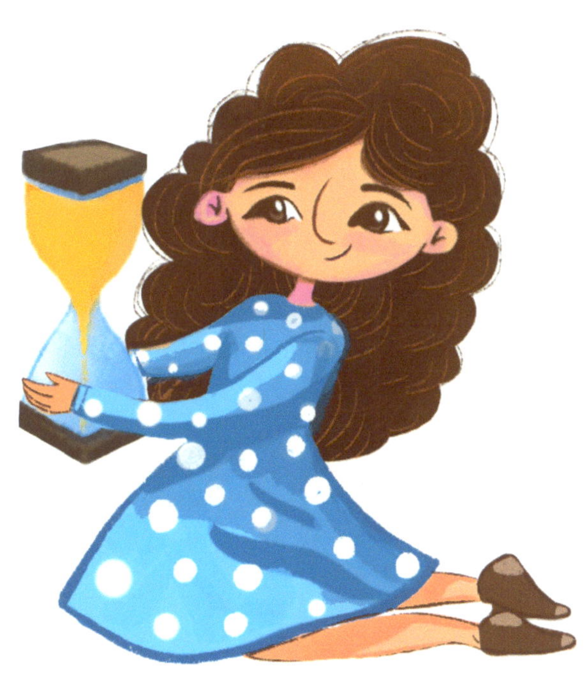

Dedications:

My son Michael, I love you. Enjoy and cherish all the memorable moments with the things and people you love! To my readers, just like sand in an hourglass, time keeps moving forward until it runs out. Make sure you're making the most of every day!

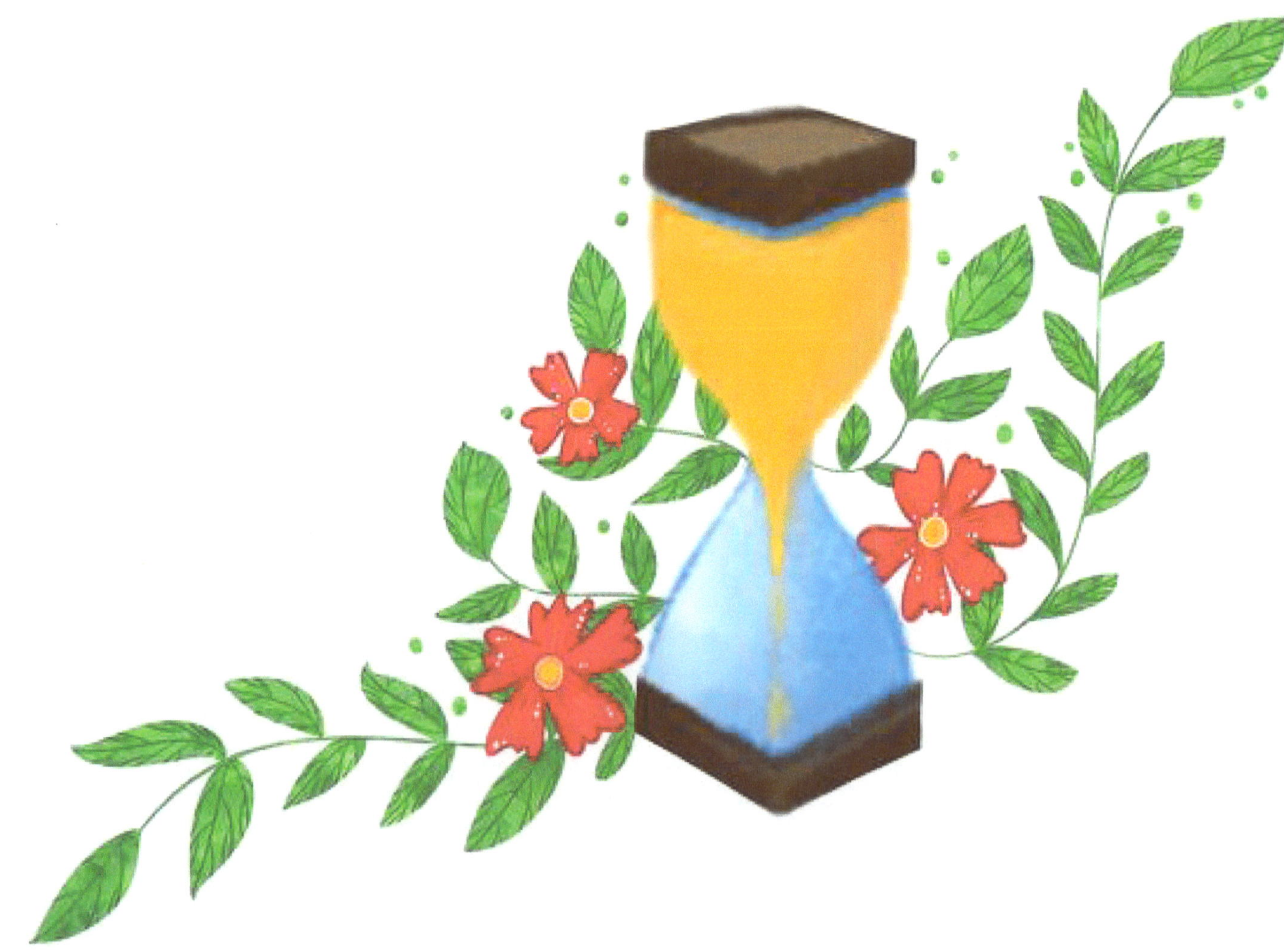

This Book Belongs To:

____

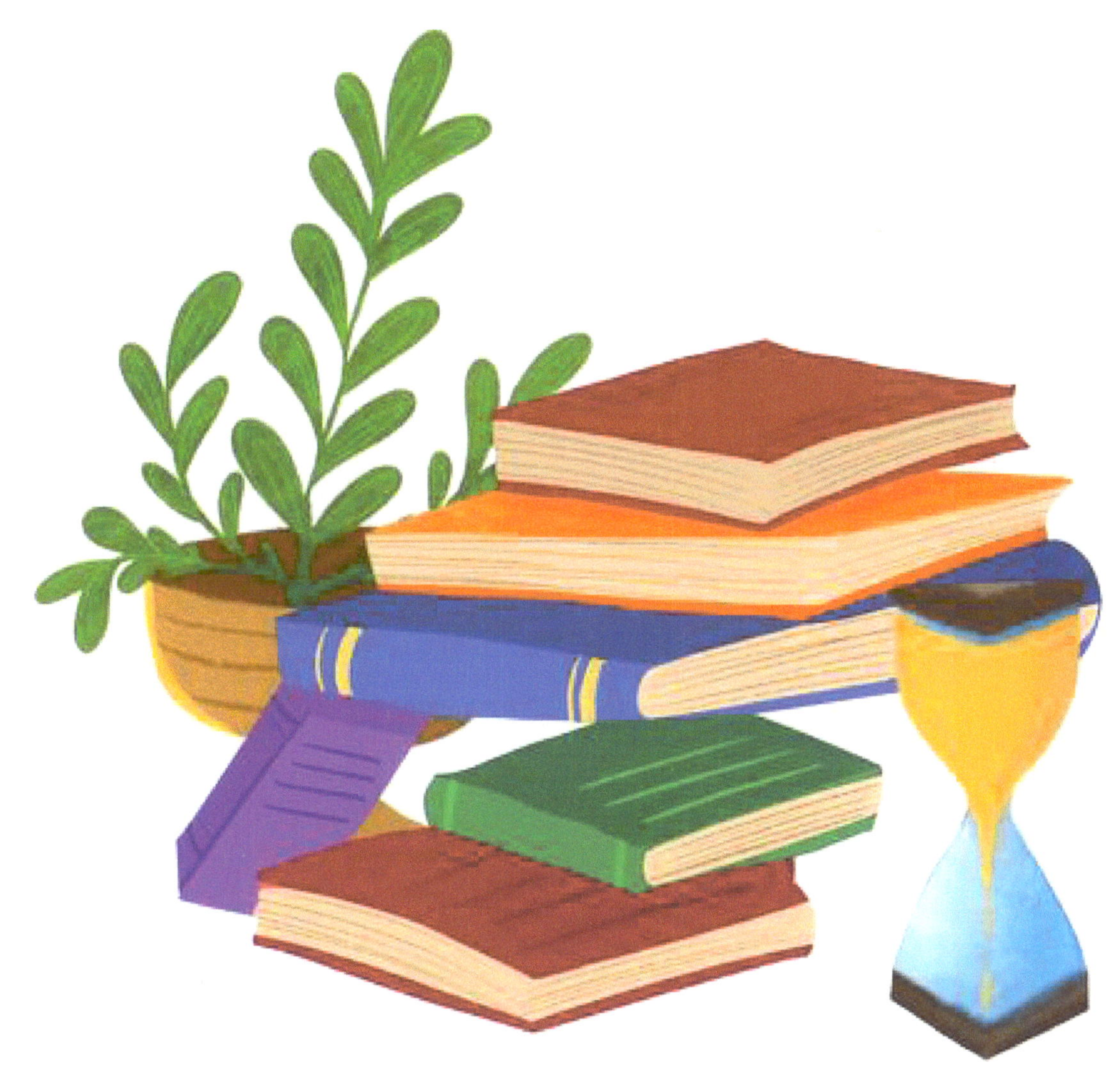

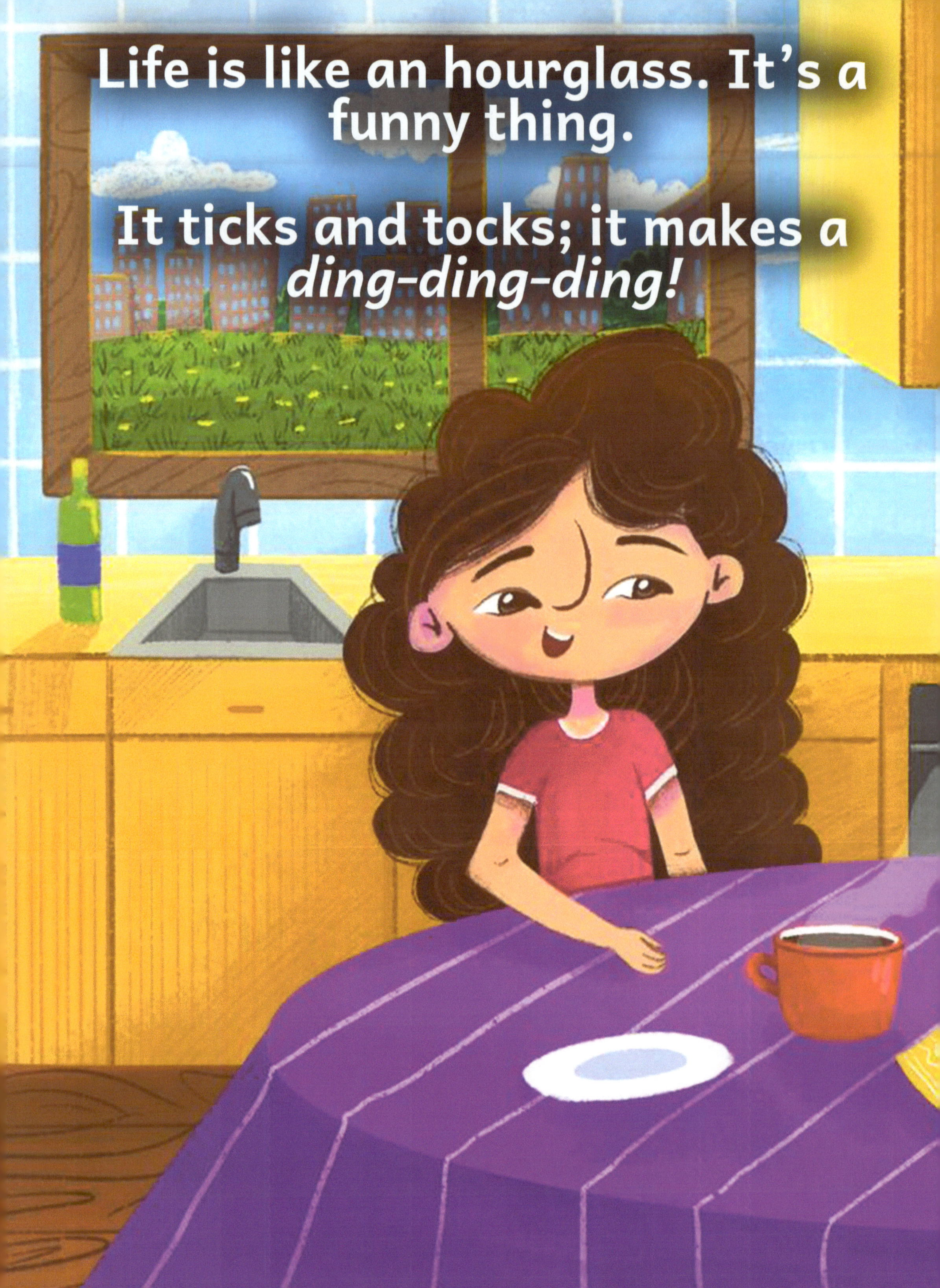

Life is like an hourglass. It's a funny thing.

It ticks and tocks; it makes a *ding-ding-ding!*

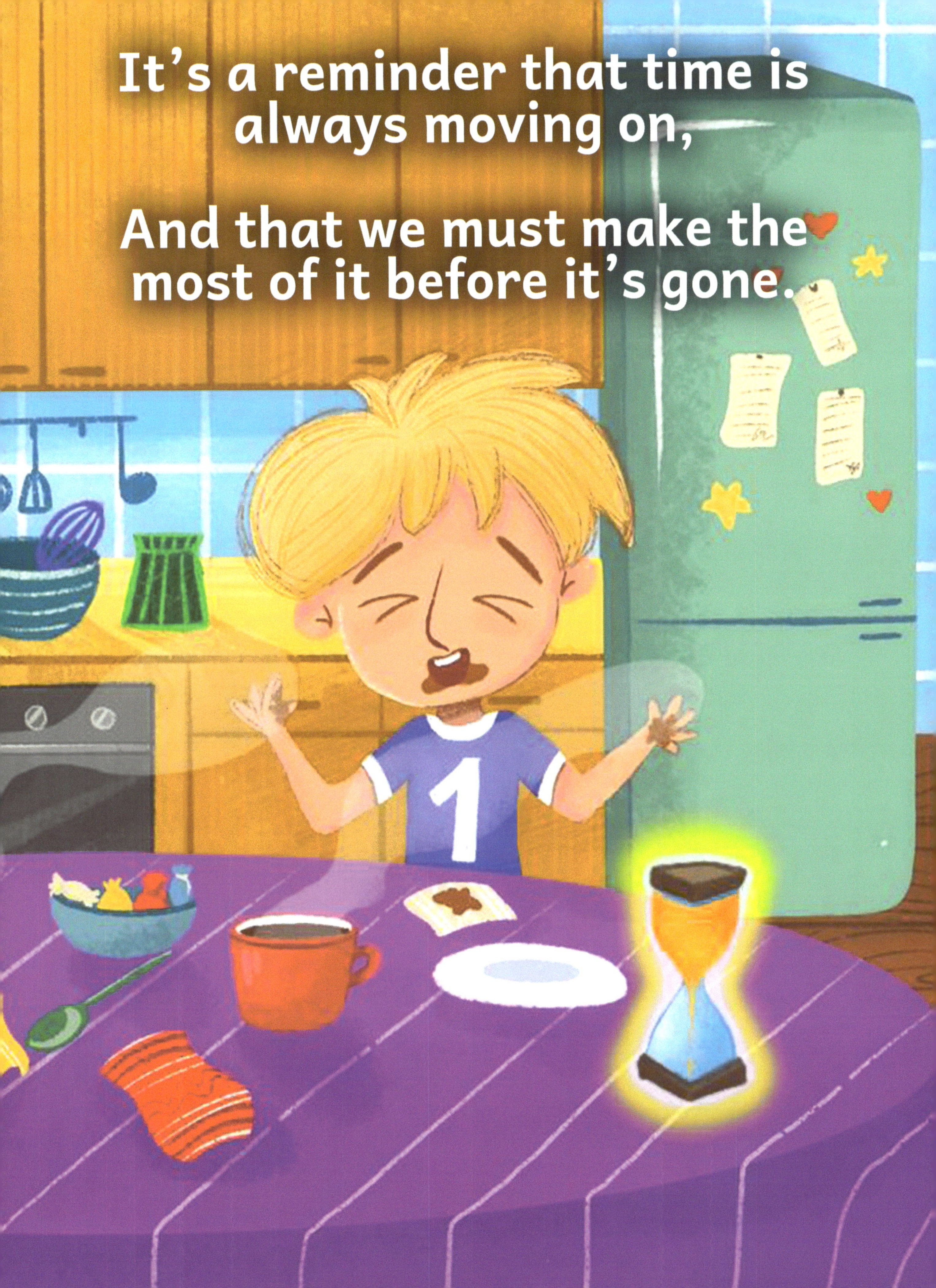

It’s a reminder that time is always moving on,

And that we must make the most of it before it’s gone.

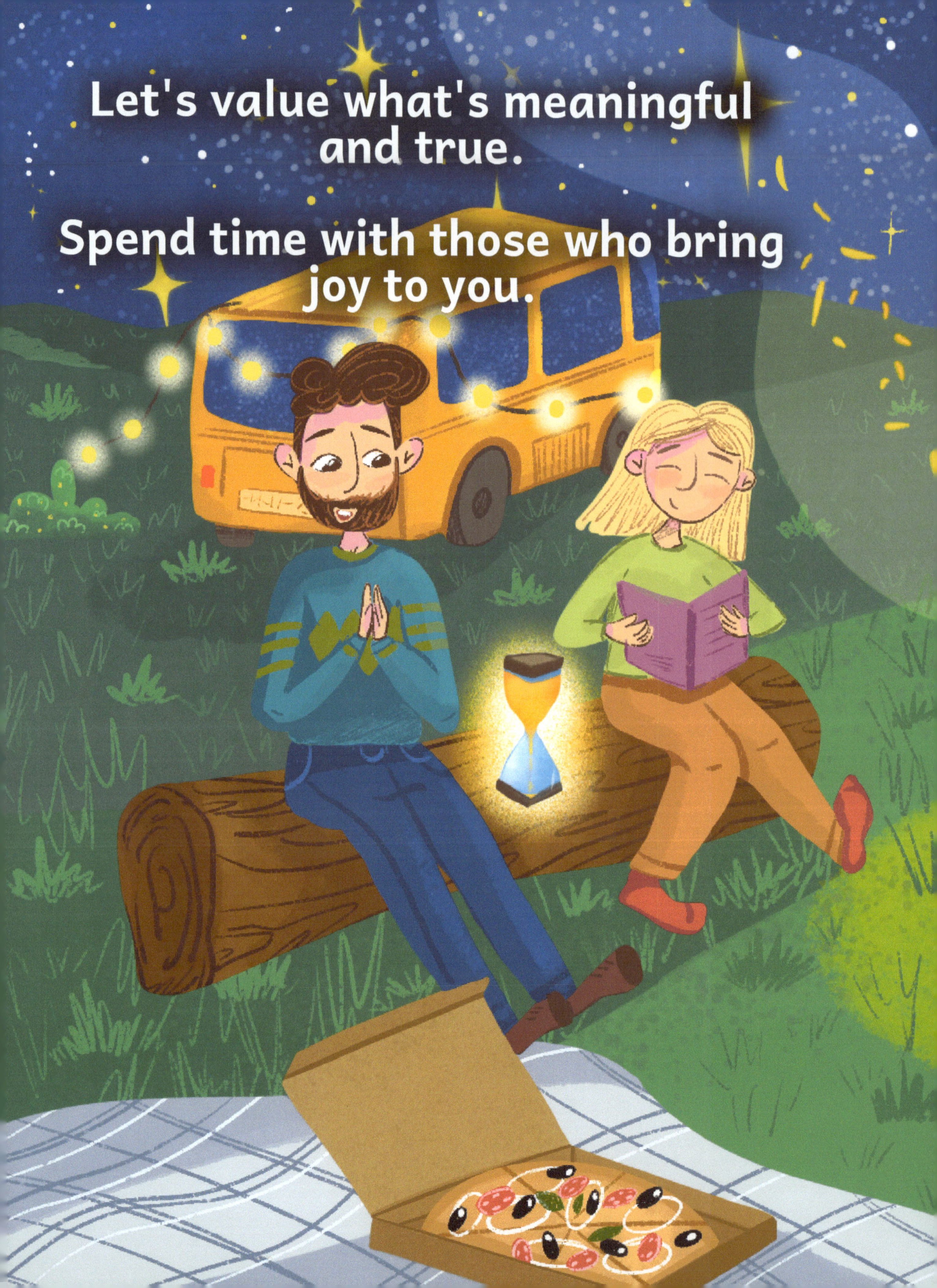
Let's value what's meaningful and true.
Spend time with those who bring joy to you.

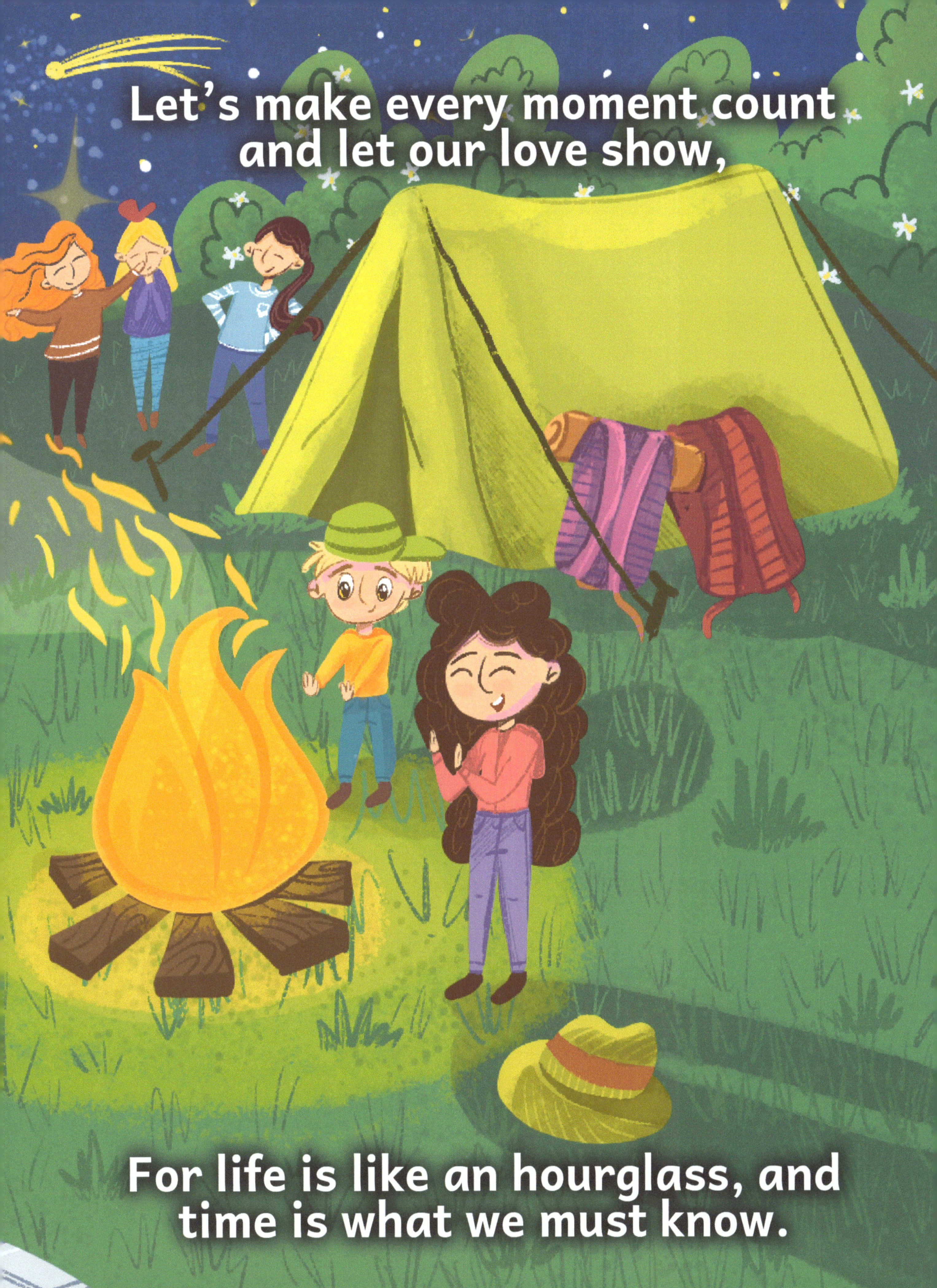
Let's make every moment count
and let our love show,
For life is like an hourglass, and
time is what we must know.

Let's be grateful for the people who stay by our side.

Let's make our journey together a beautiful ride.

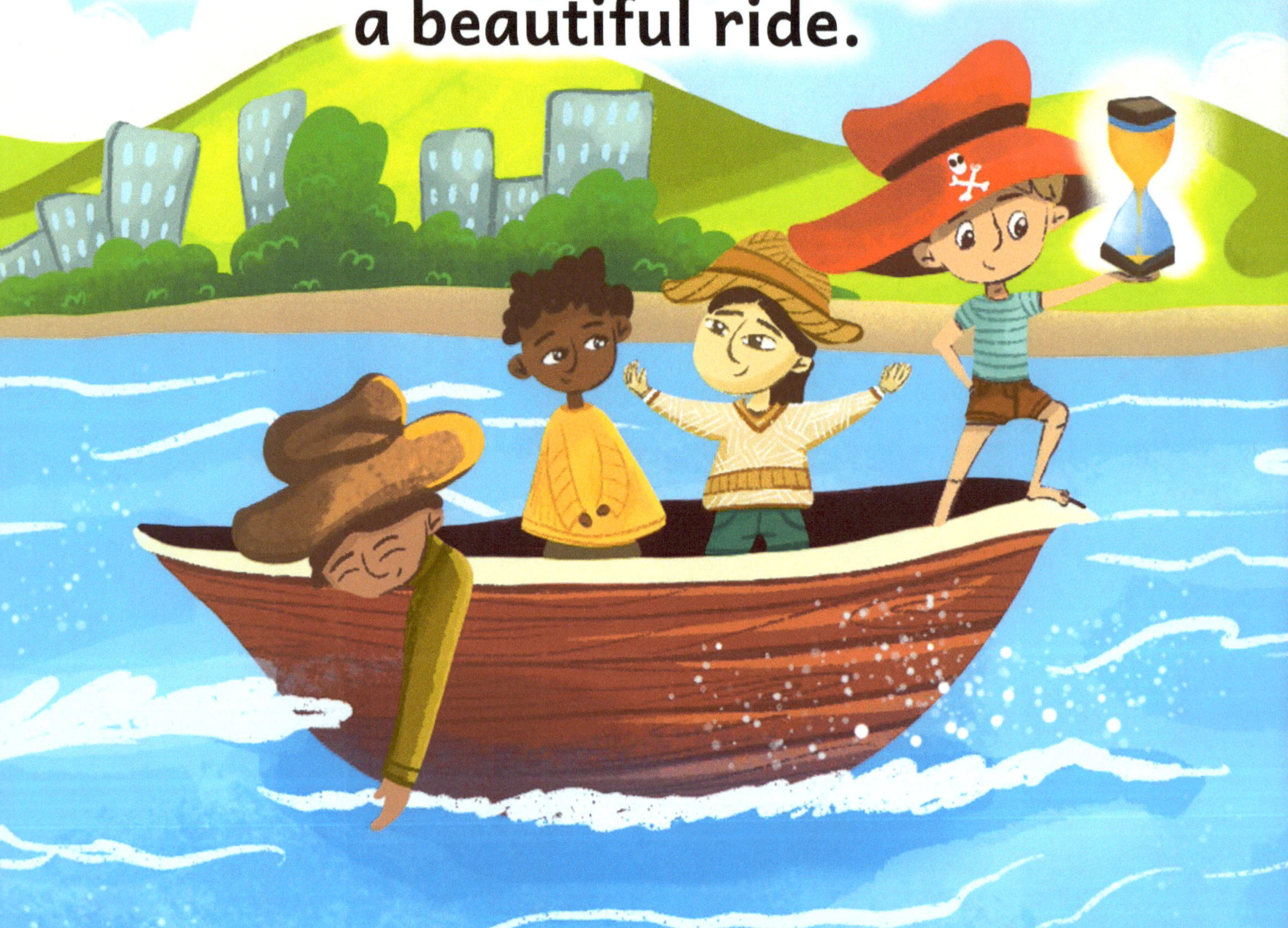

For life is like an hourglass, and time is fleeting fast,

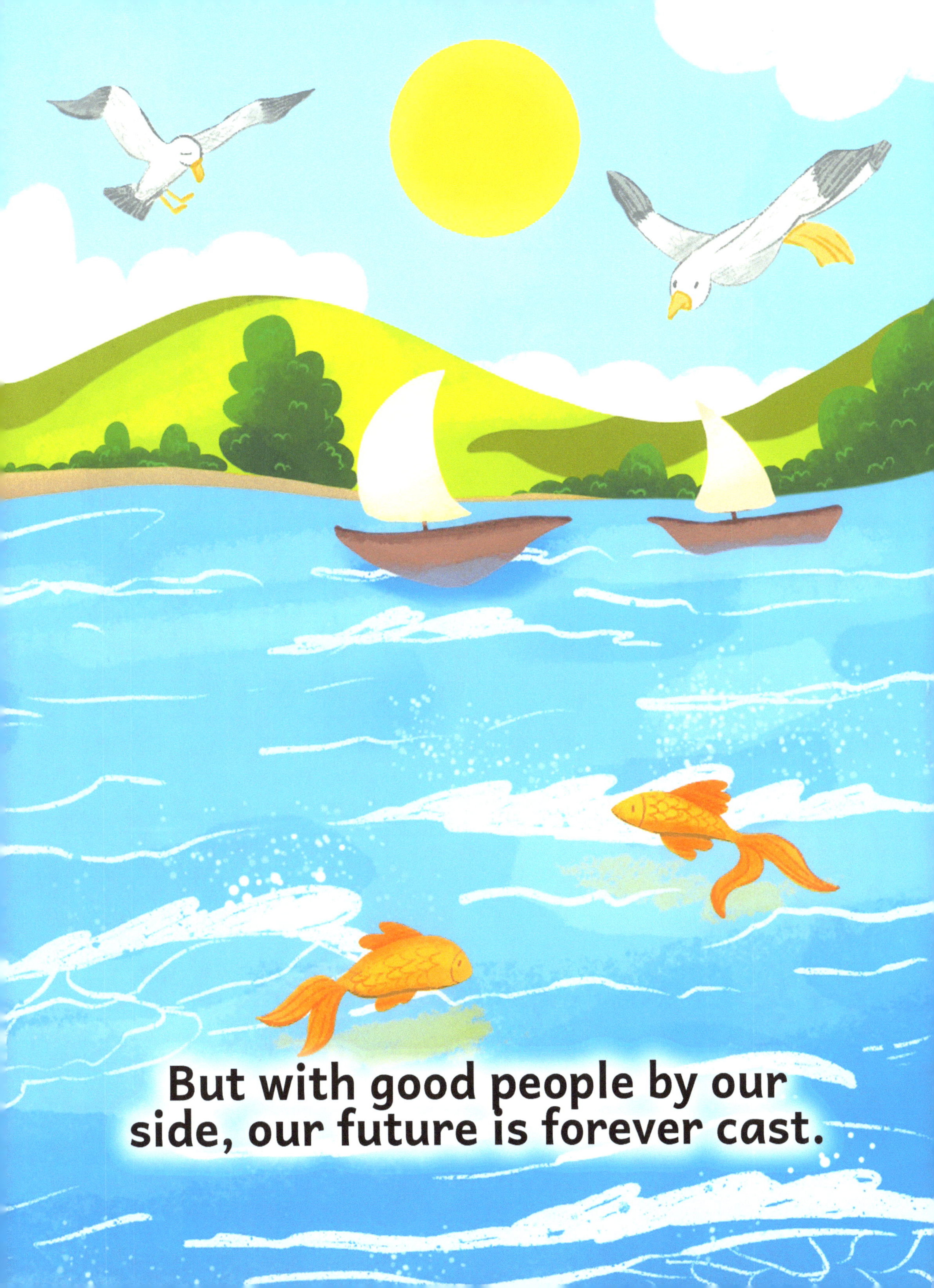

But with good people by our side, our future is forever cast.

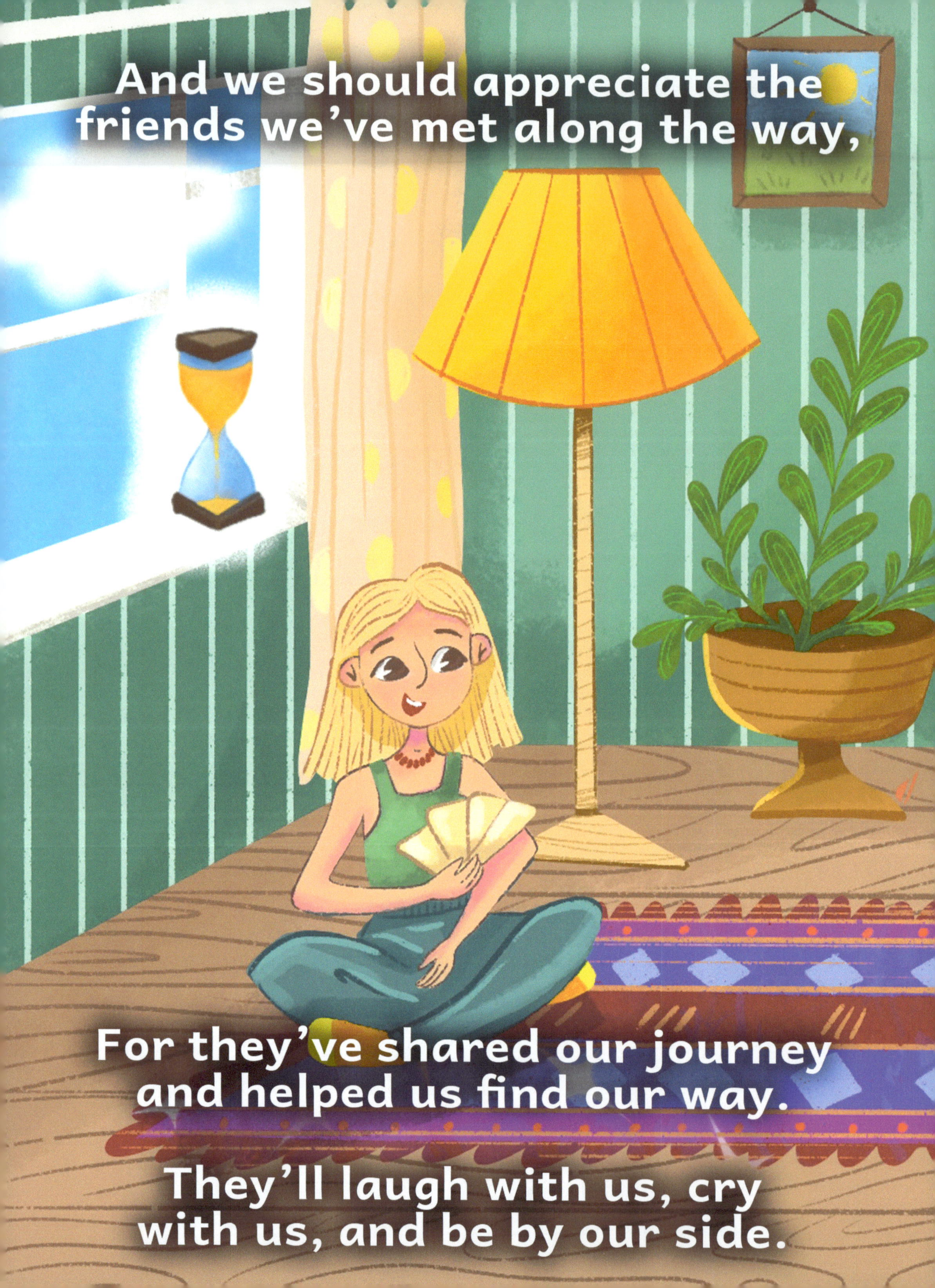

And we should appreciate the friends we've met along the way,

For they've shared our journey and helped us find our way.

They'll laugh with us, cry with us, and be by our side.

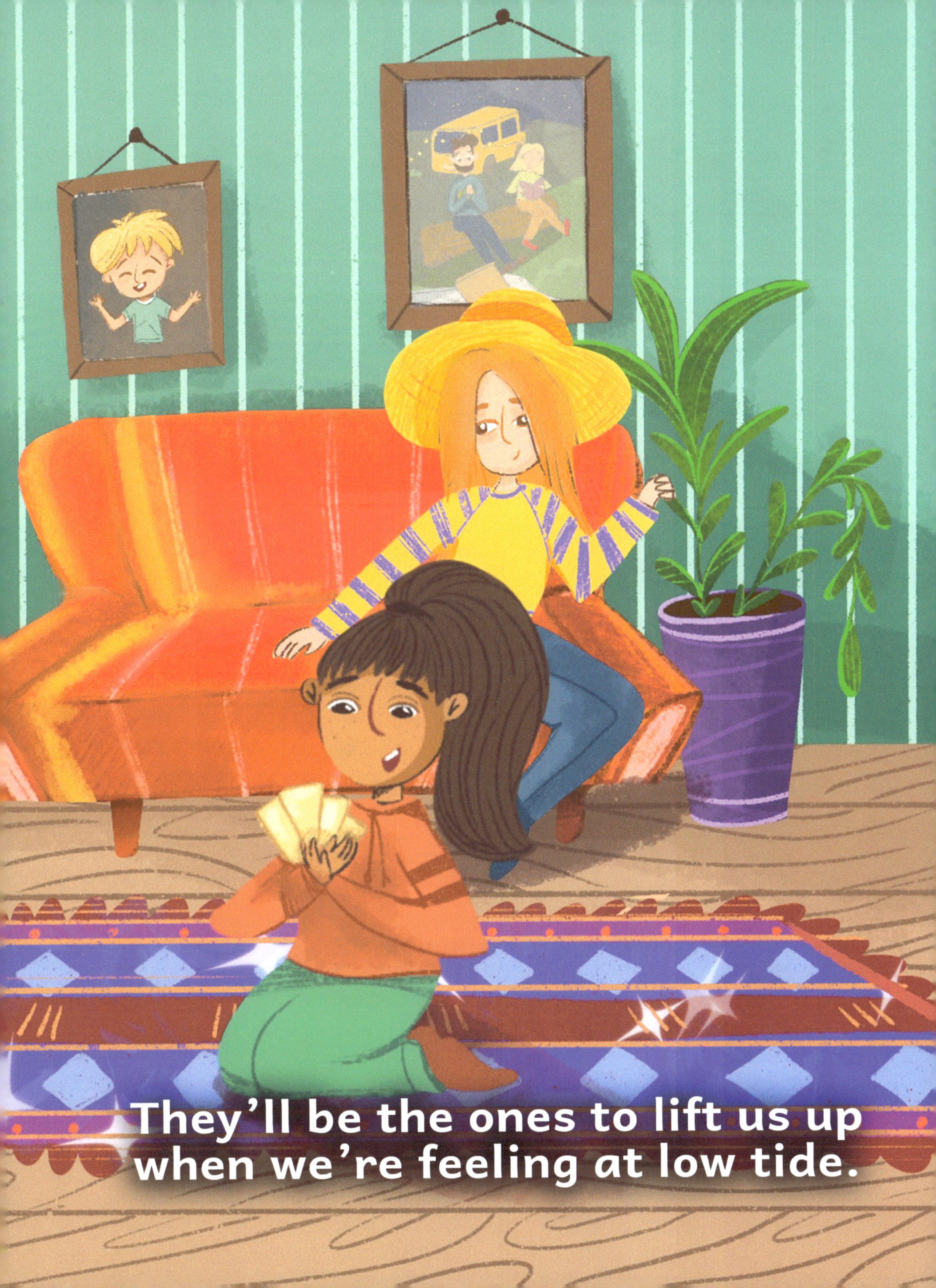

They'll be the ones to lift us up
when we're feeling at low tide.

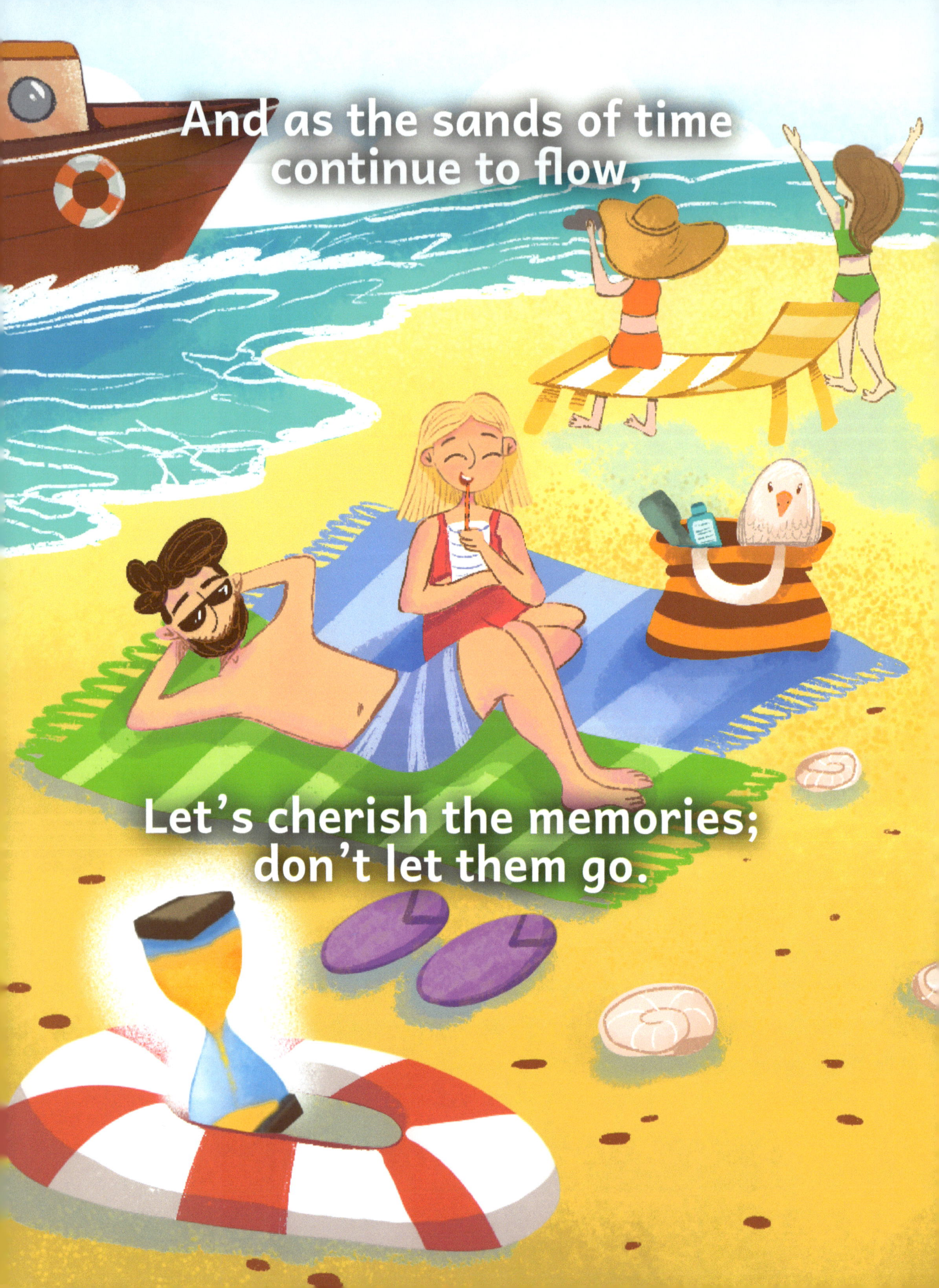
And as the sands of time
continue to flow,
Let's cherish the memories;
don't let them go.

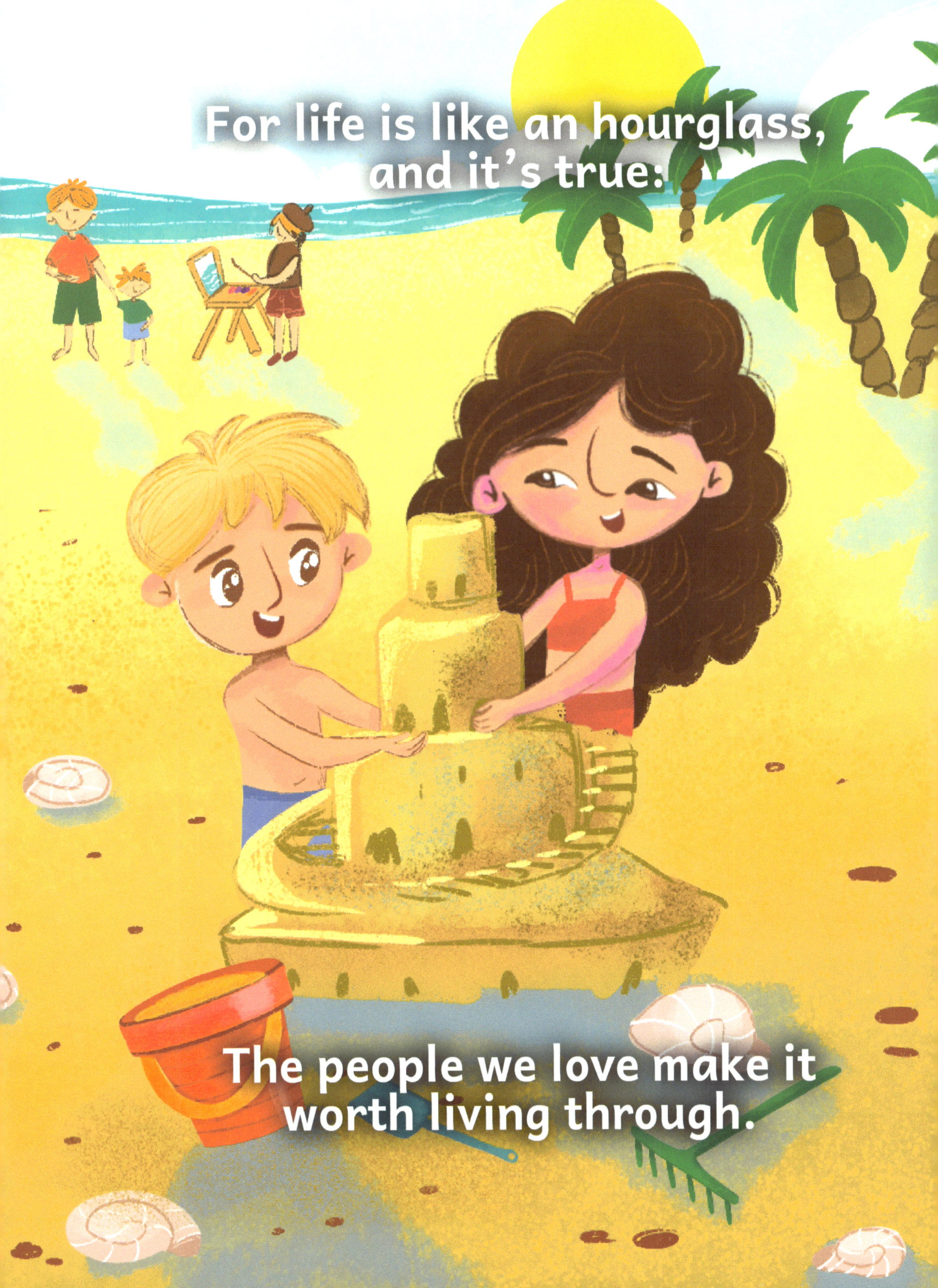

For life is like an hourglass,
and it's true:

The people we love make it
worth living through.

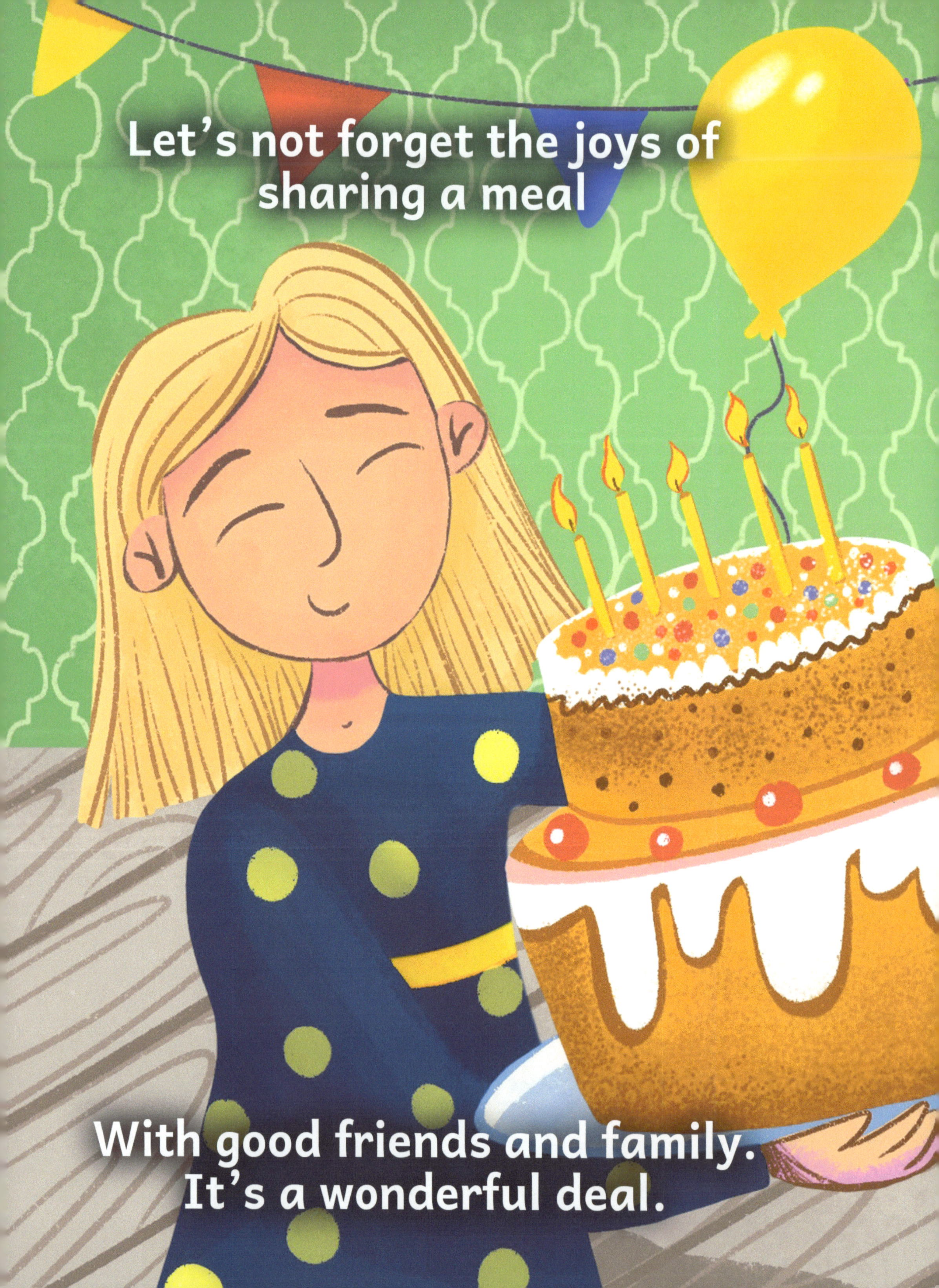
Let’s not forget the joys of
sharing a meal
With good friends and family.
It’s a wonderful deal.

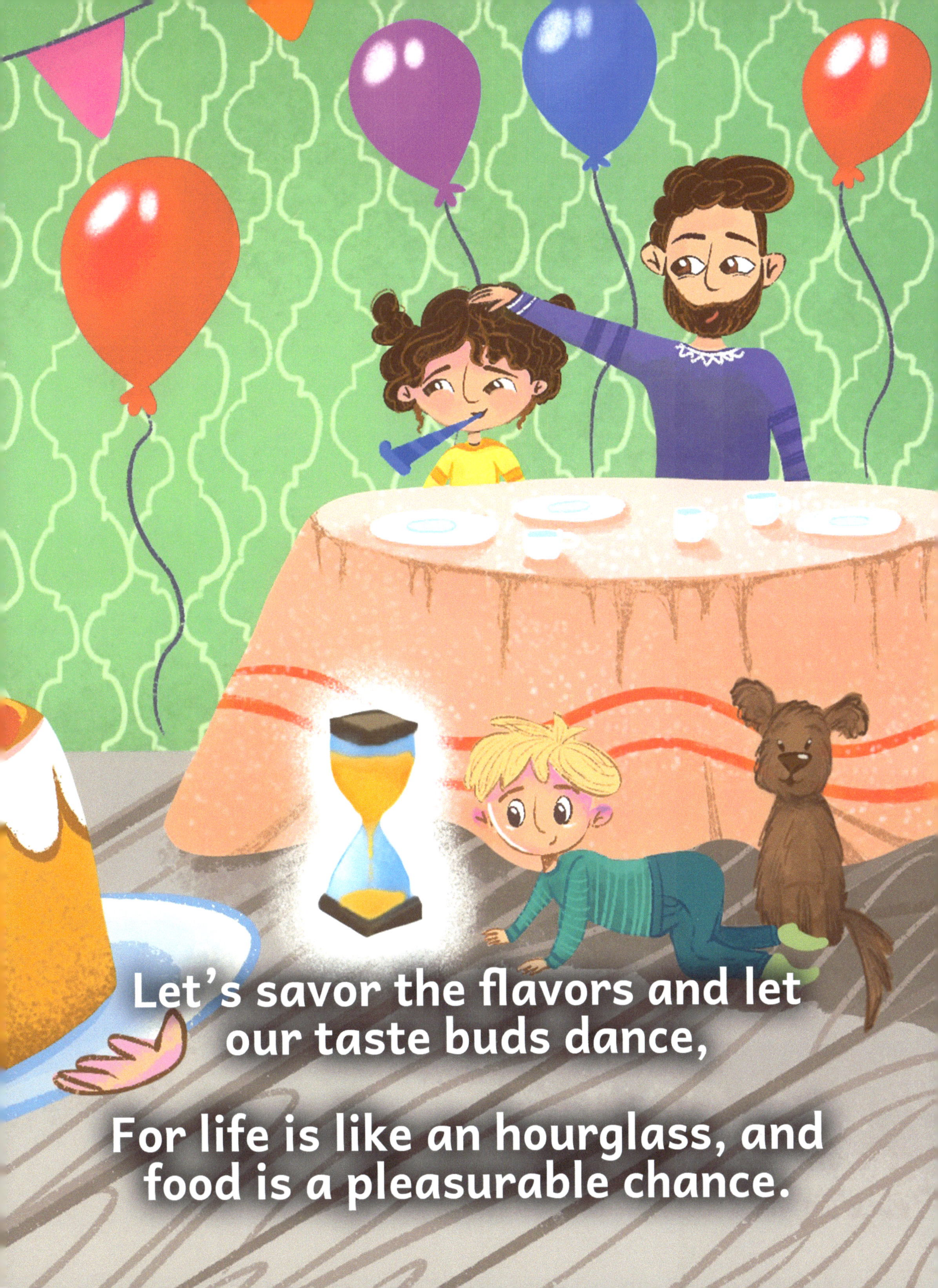

Let's savor the flavors and let our taste buds dance,

For life is like an hourglass, and food is a pleasurable chance.

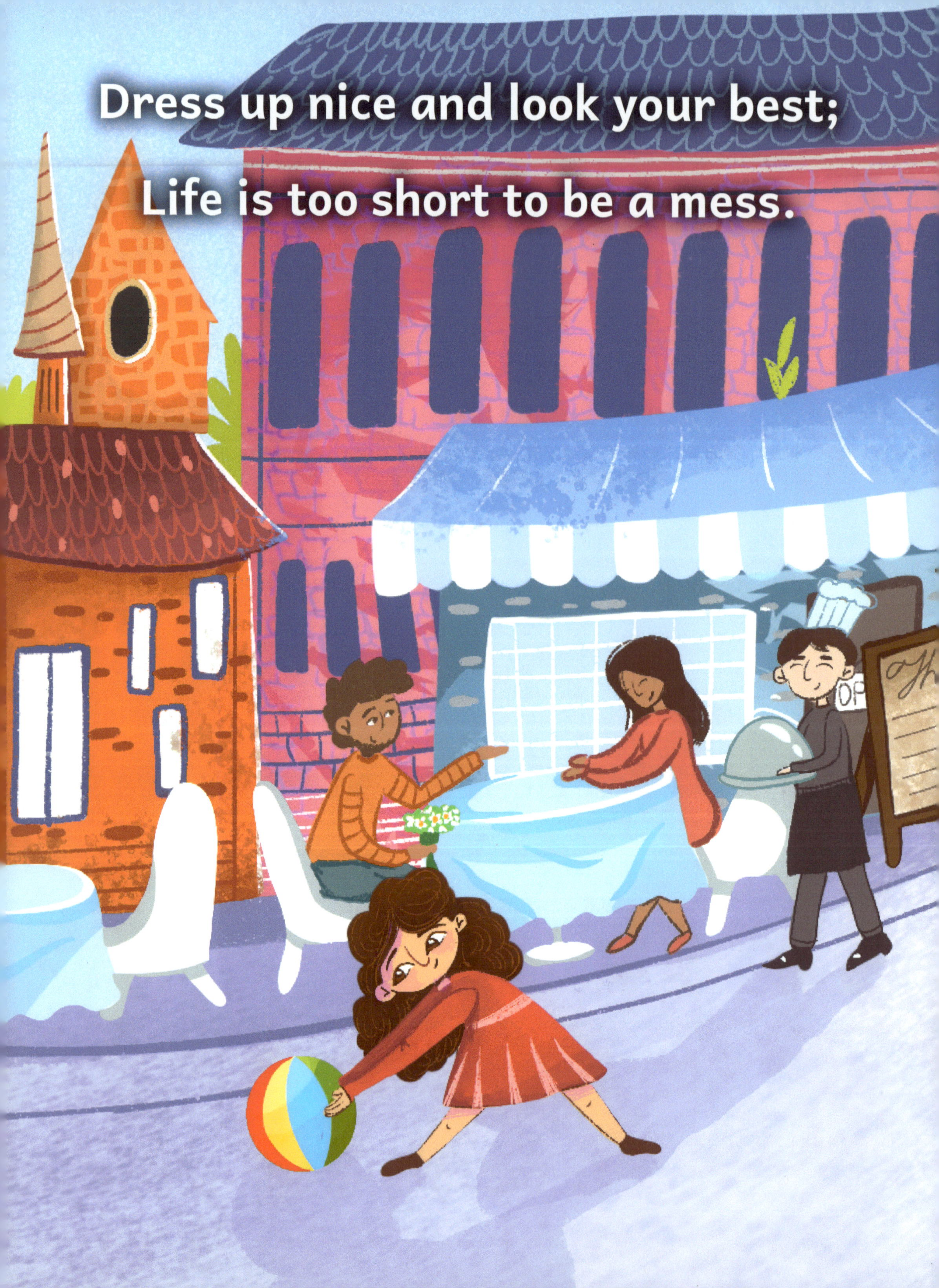

Dress up nice and look your best;

Life is too short to be a mess.

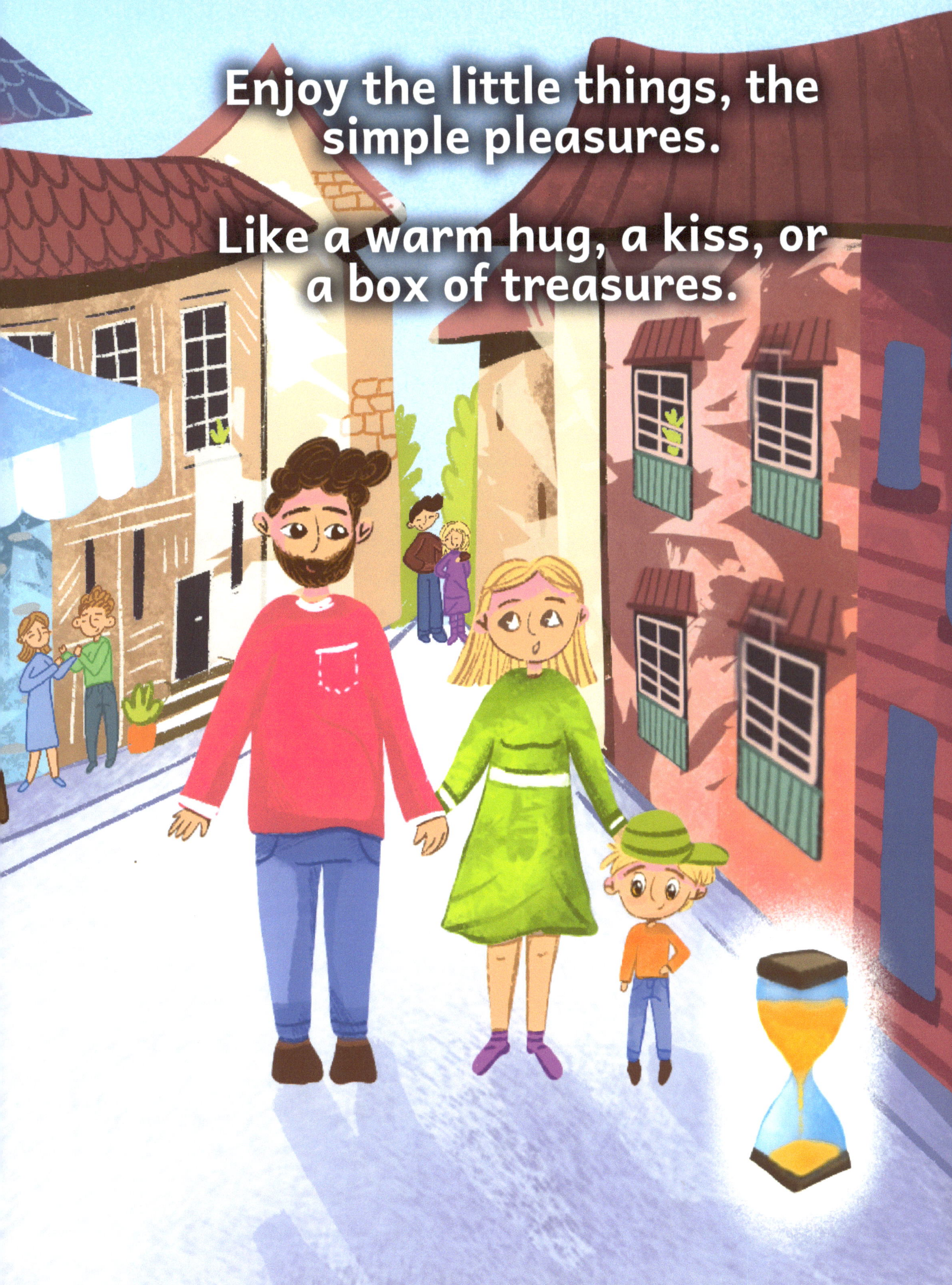

Enjoy the little things, the simple pleasures.

Like a warm hug, a kiss, or a box of treasures.

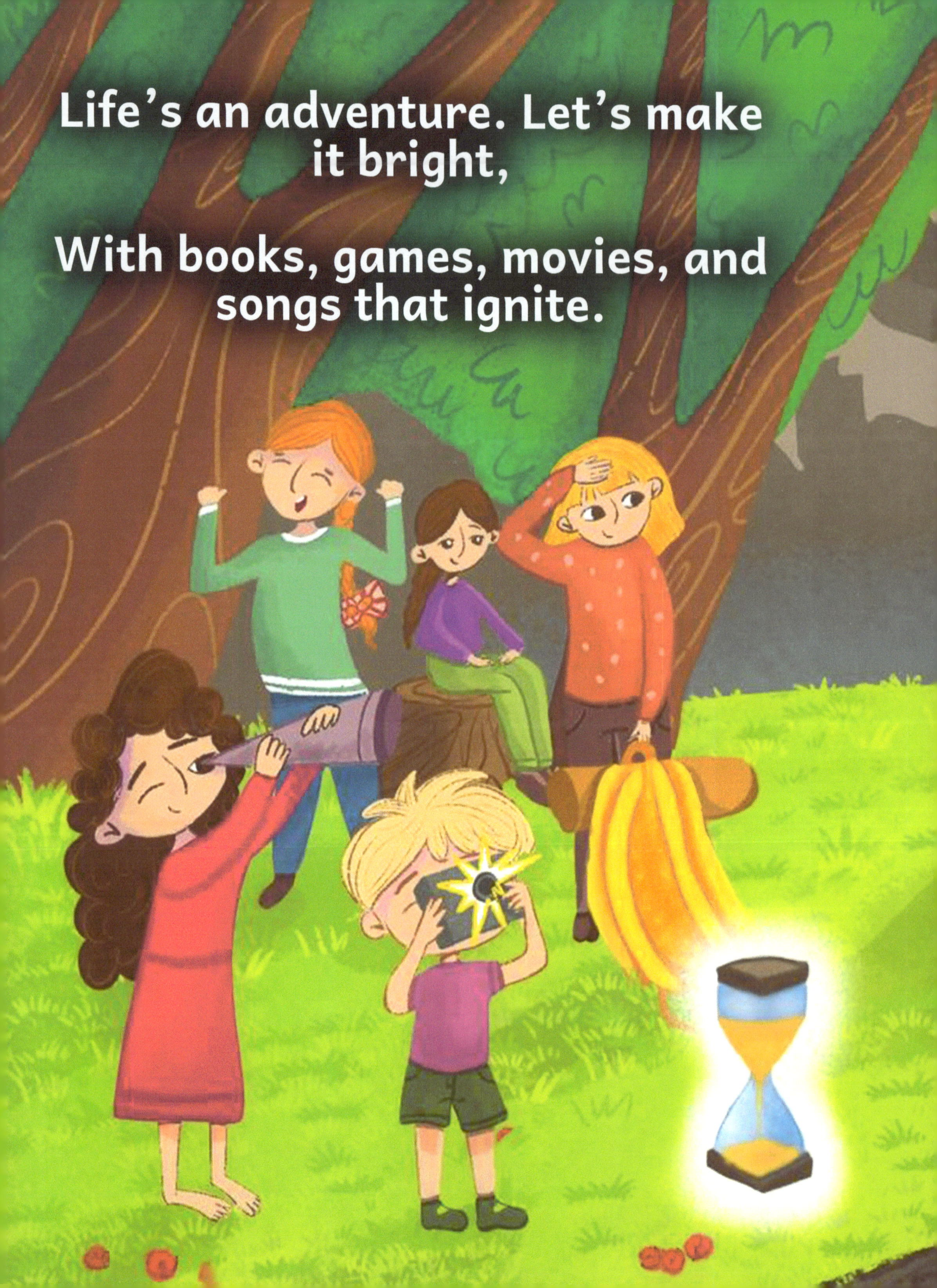
Life's an adventure. Let's make it bright,

With books, games, movies, and songs that ignite.

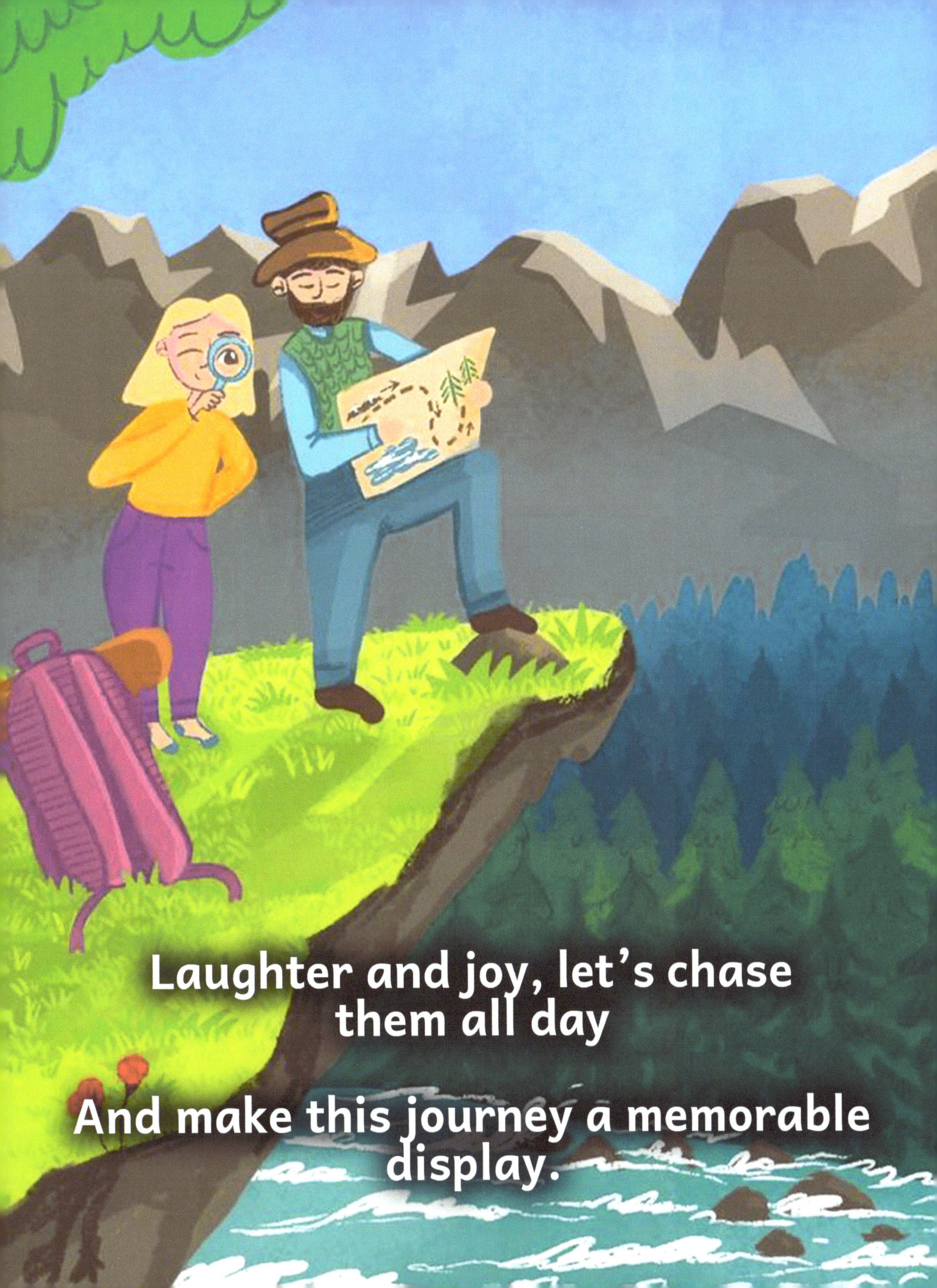

Laughter and joy, let's chase them all day

And make this journey a memorable display.

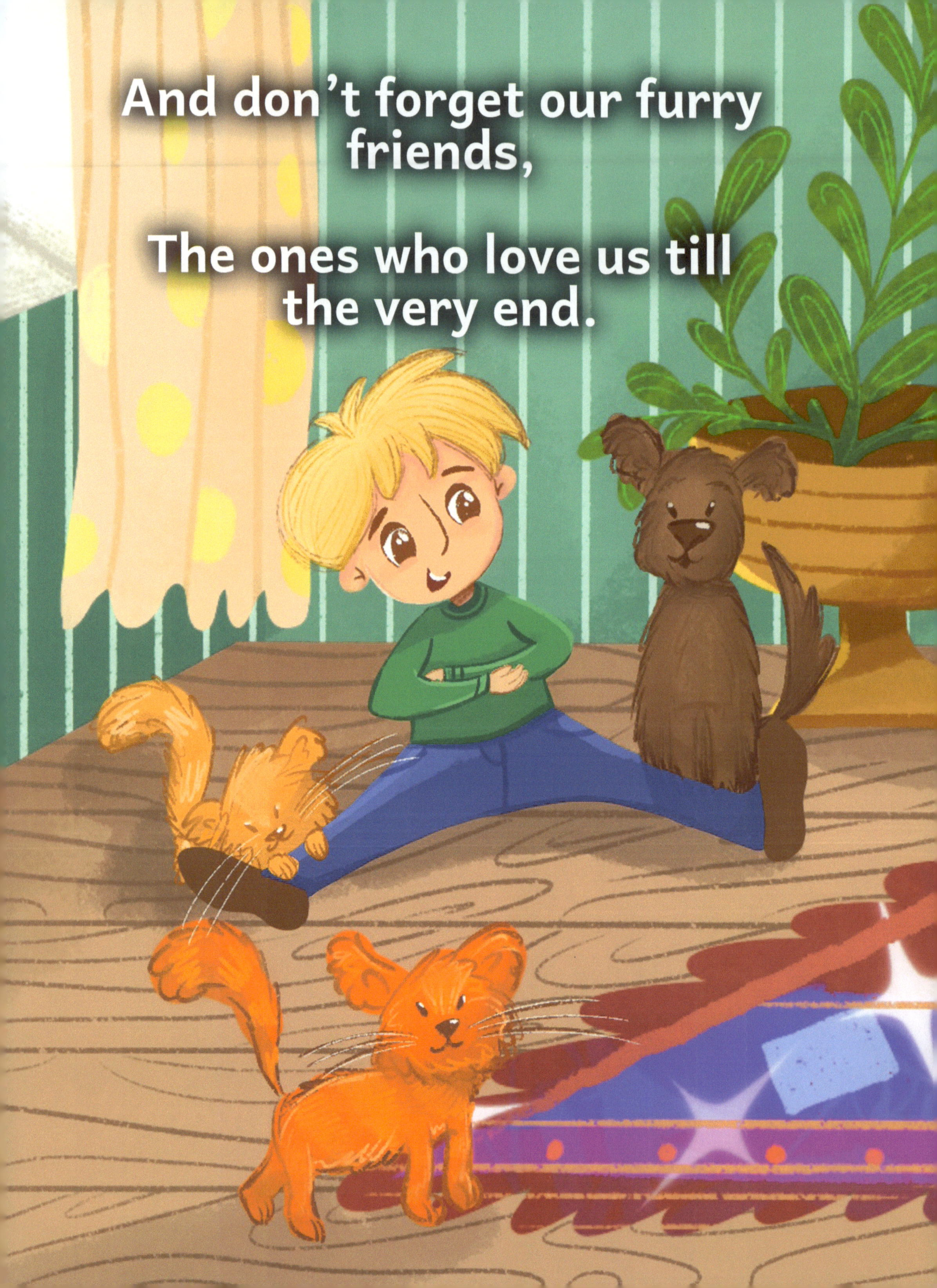

And don't forget our furry friends,

The ones who love us till the very end.

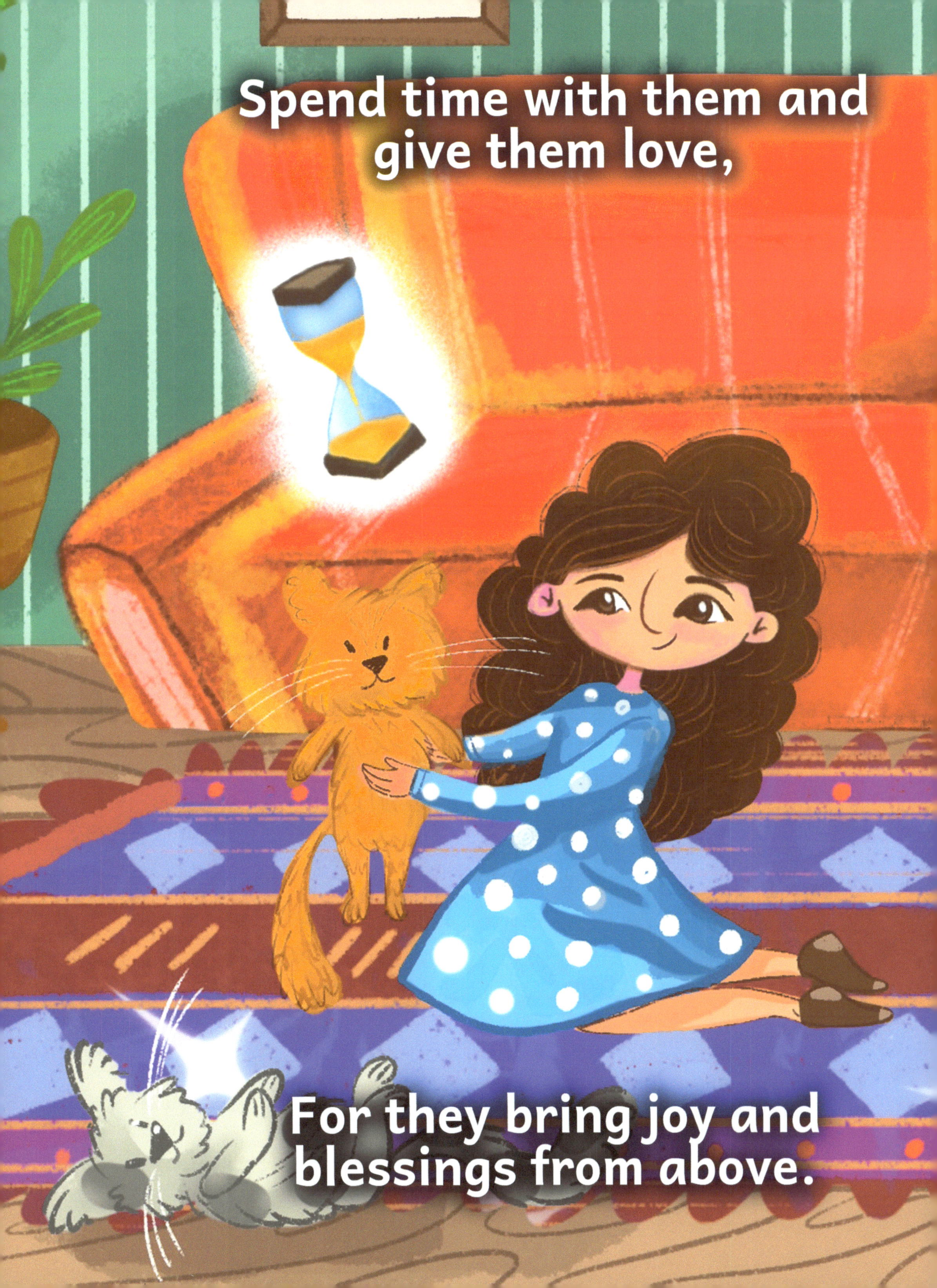
Spend time with them and
give them love,
For they bring joy and
blessings from above.

Let's explore the world and
let our minds open wide,

For life is like an hourglass,
and it's worth taking a ride.

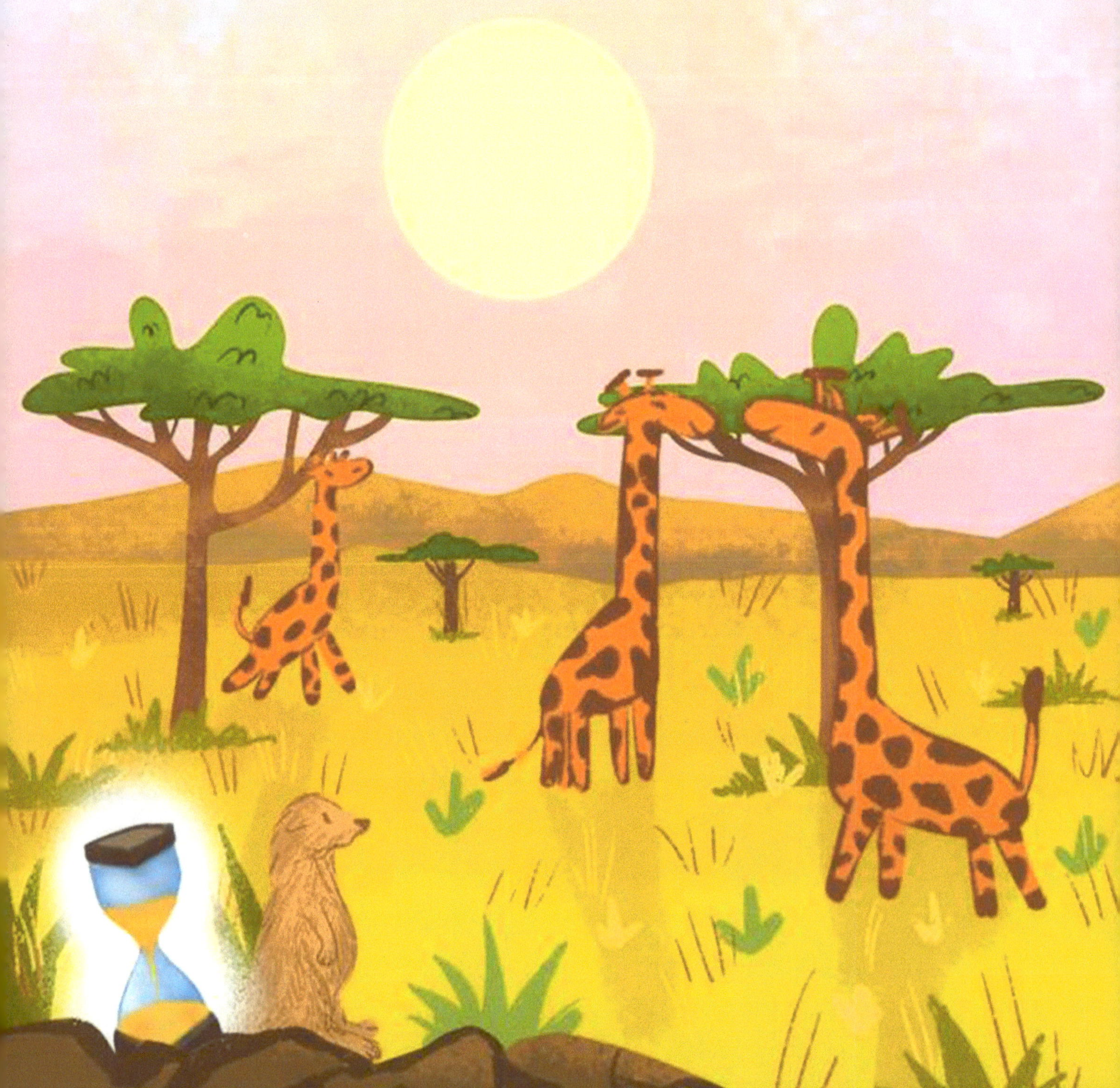

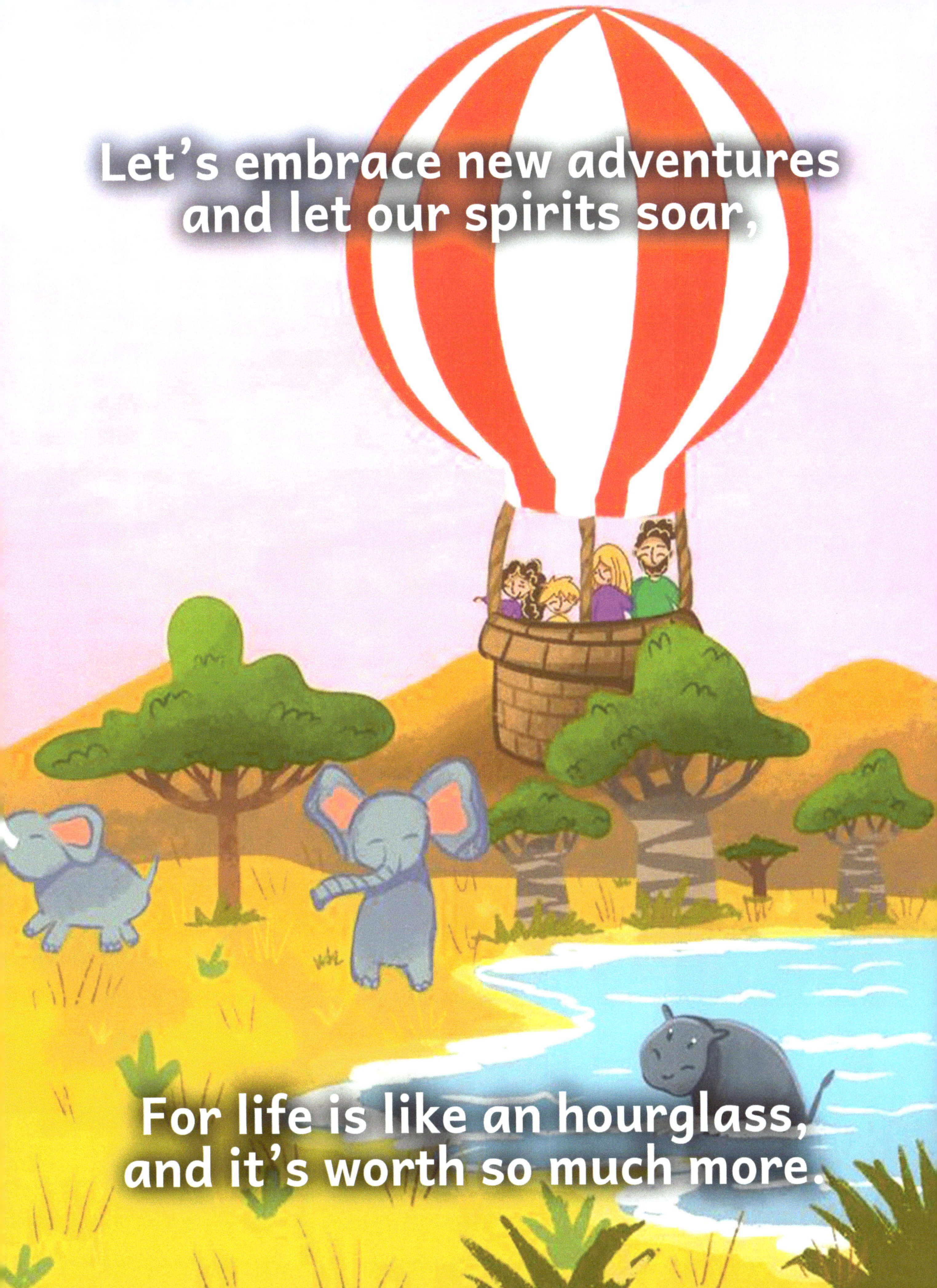

Let's embrace new adventures
and let our spirits soar,

For life is like an hourglass,
and it's worth so much more.

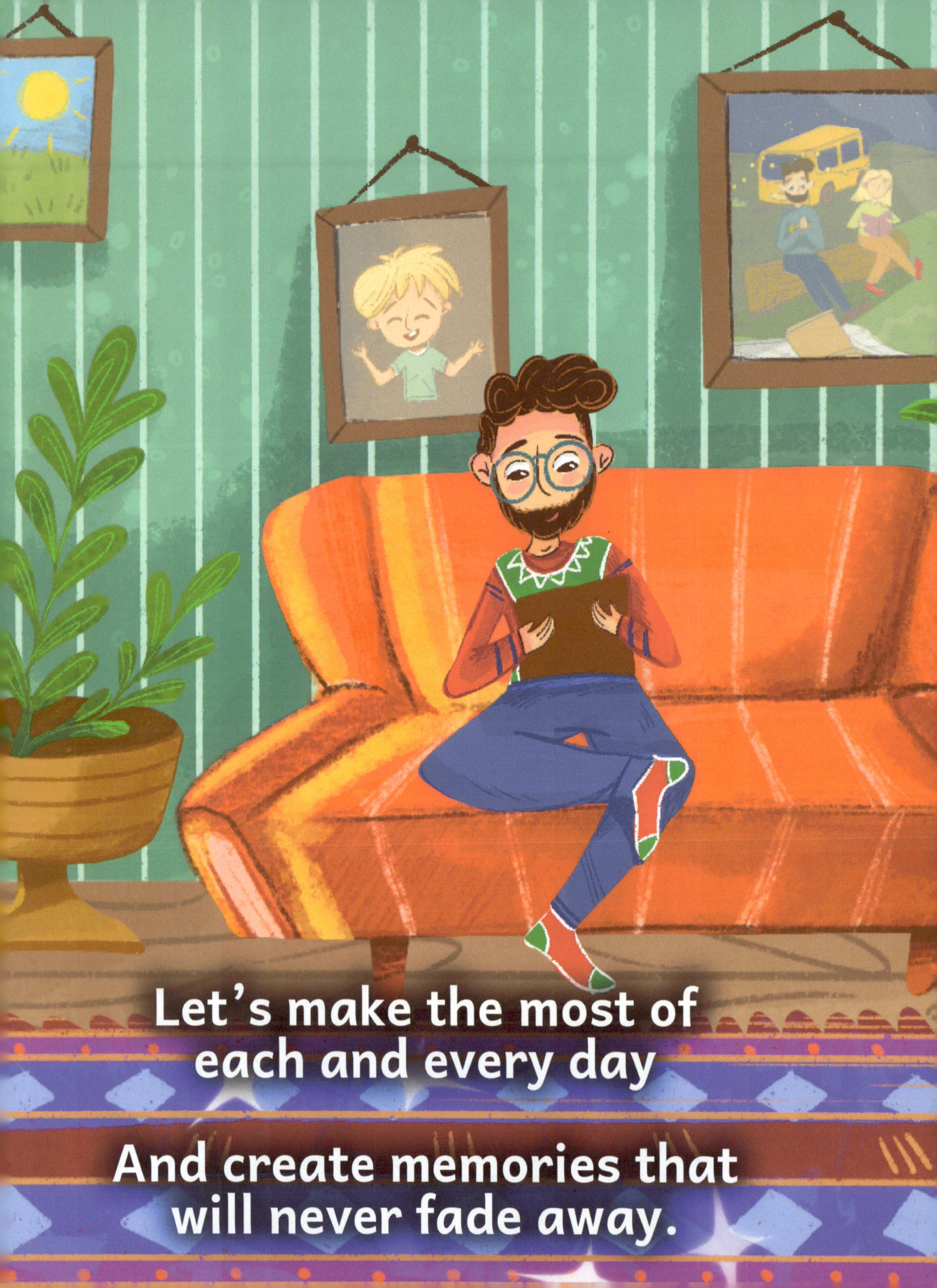

Let's make the most of
each and every day

And create memories that
will never fade away.

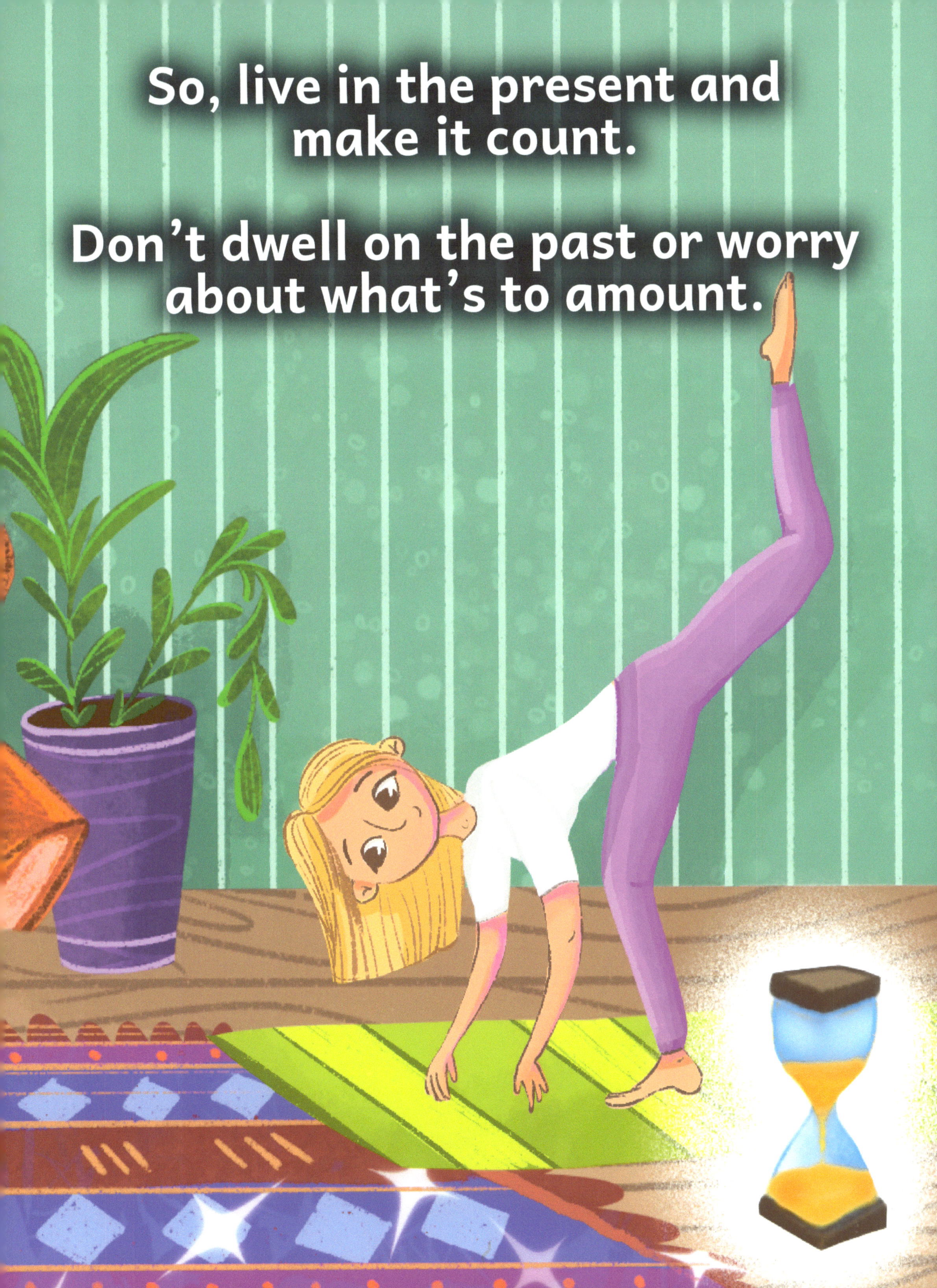
So, live in the present and make it count.
Don't dwell on the past or worry about what's to amount.

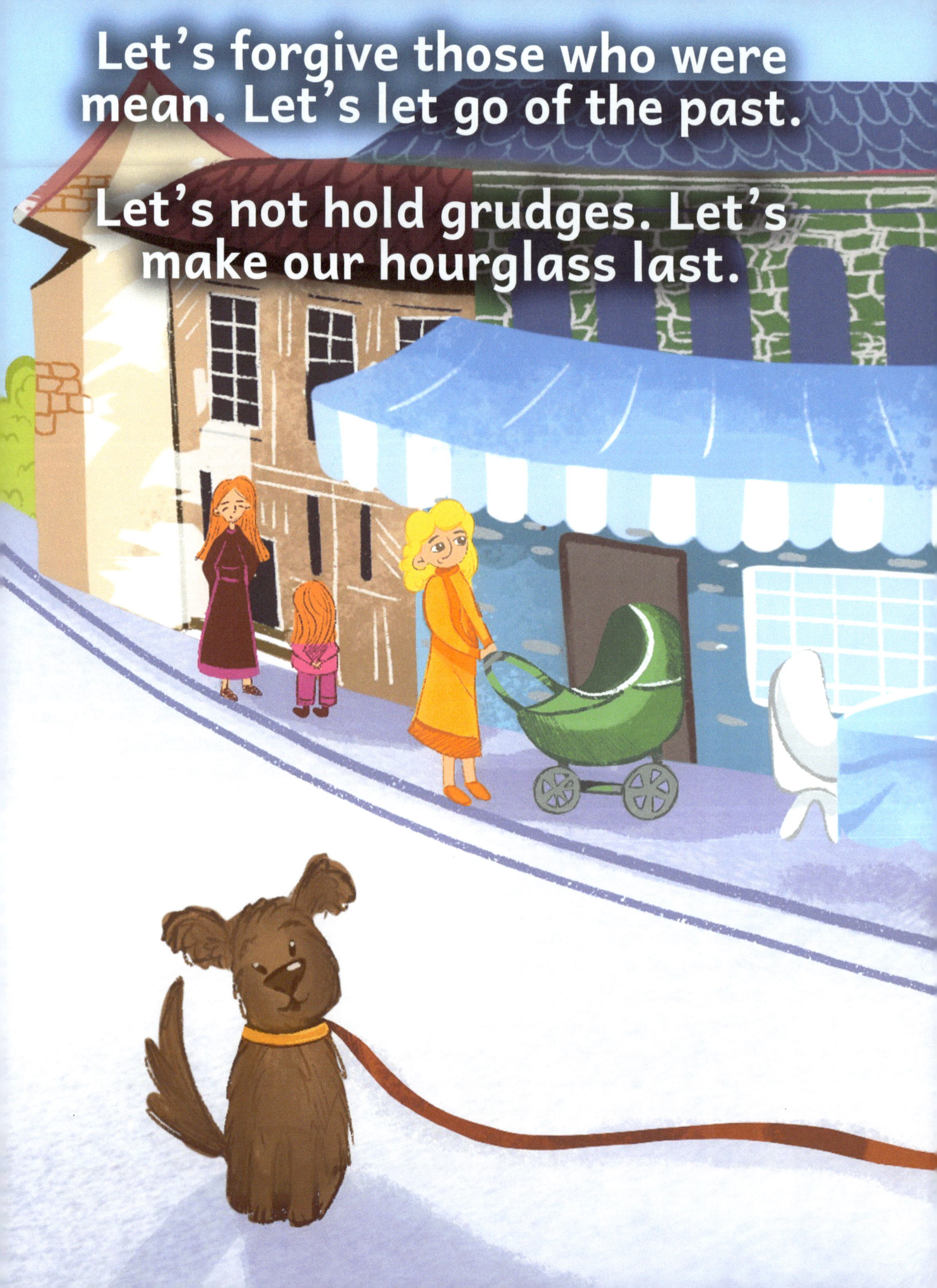

Let’s forgive those who were mean. Let’s let go of the past.

Let’s not hold grudges. Let’s make our hourglass last.

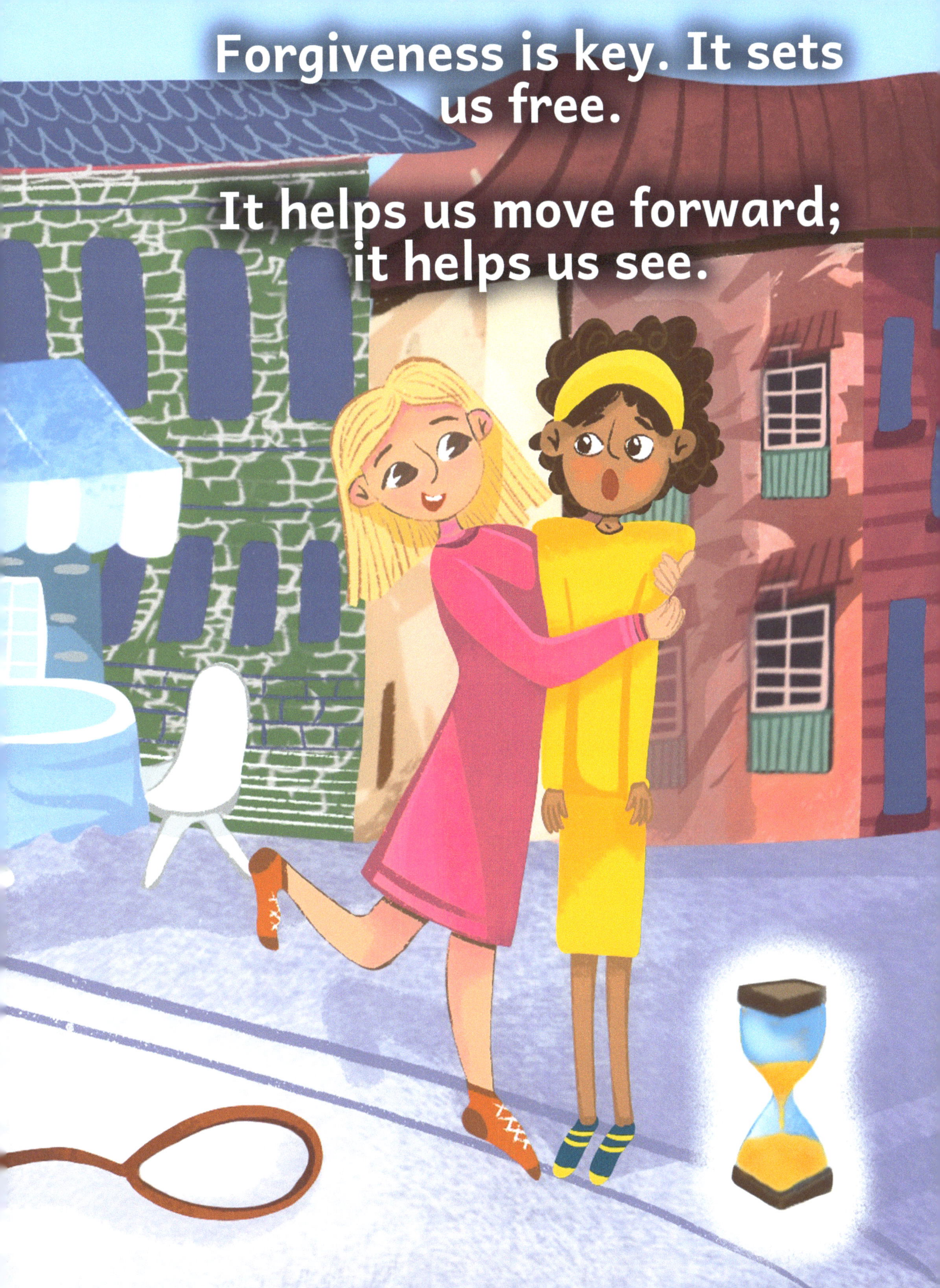

Forgiveness is key. It sets us free.

It helps us move forward; it helps us see.

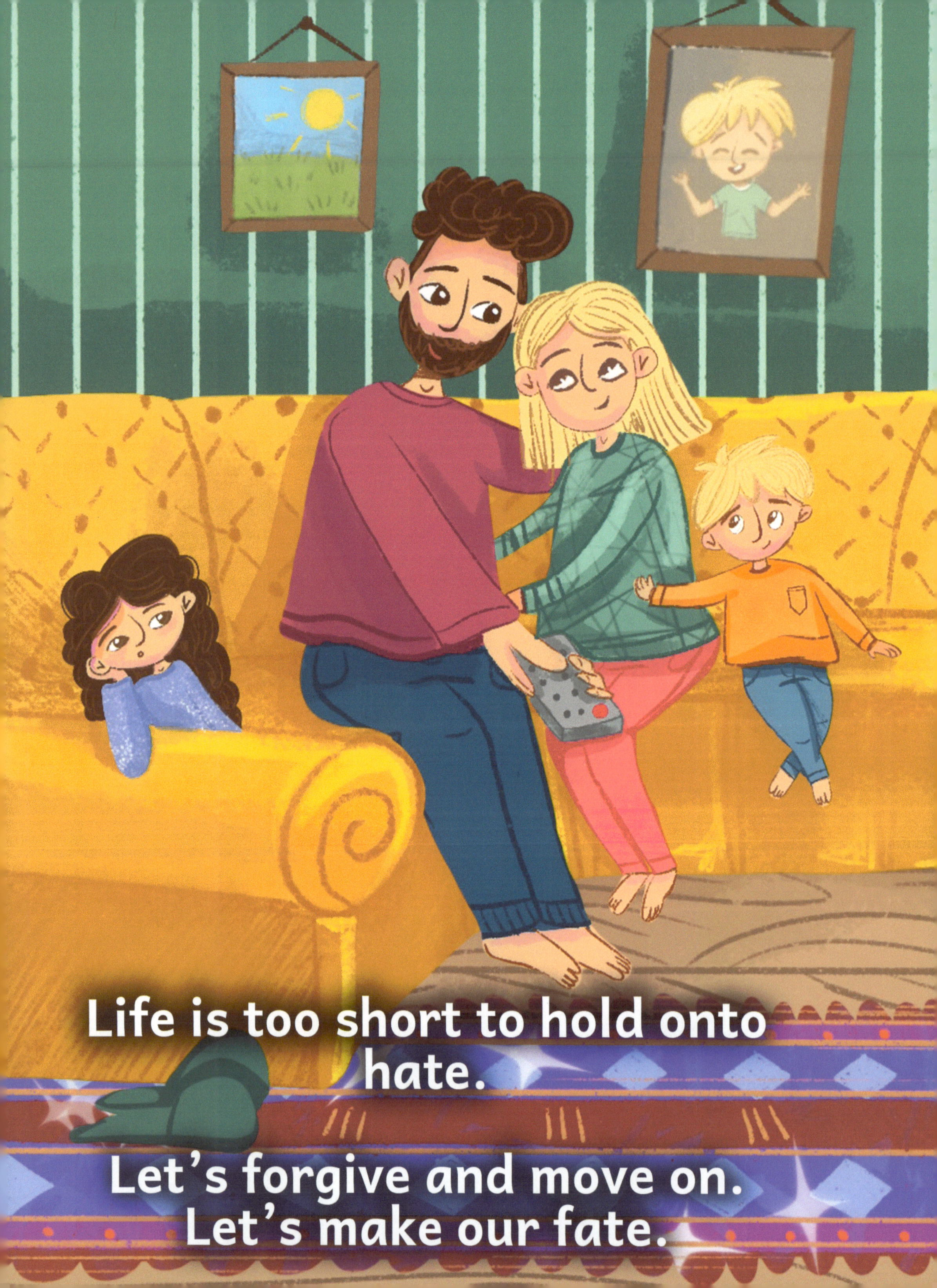
Life is too short to hold onto hate.
Let's forgive and move on. Let's make our fate.

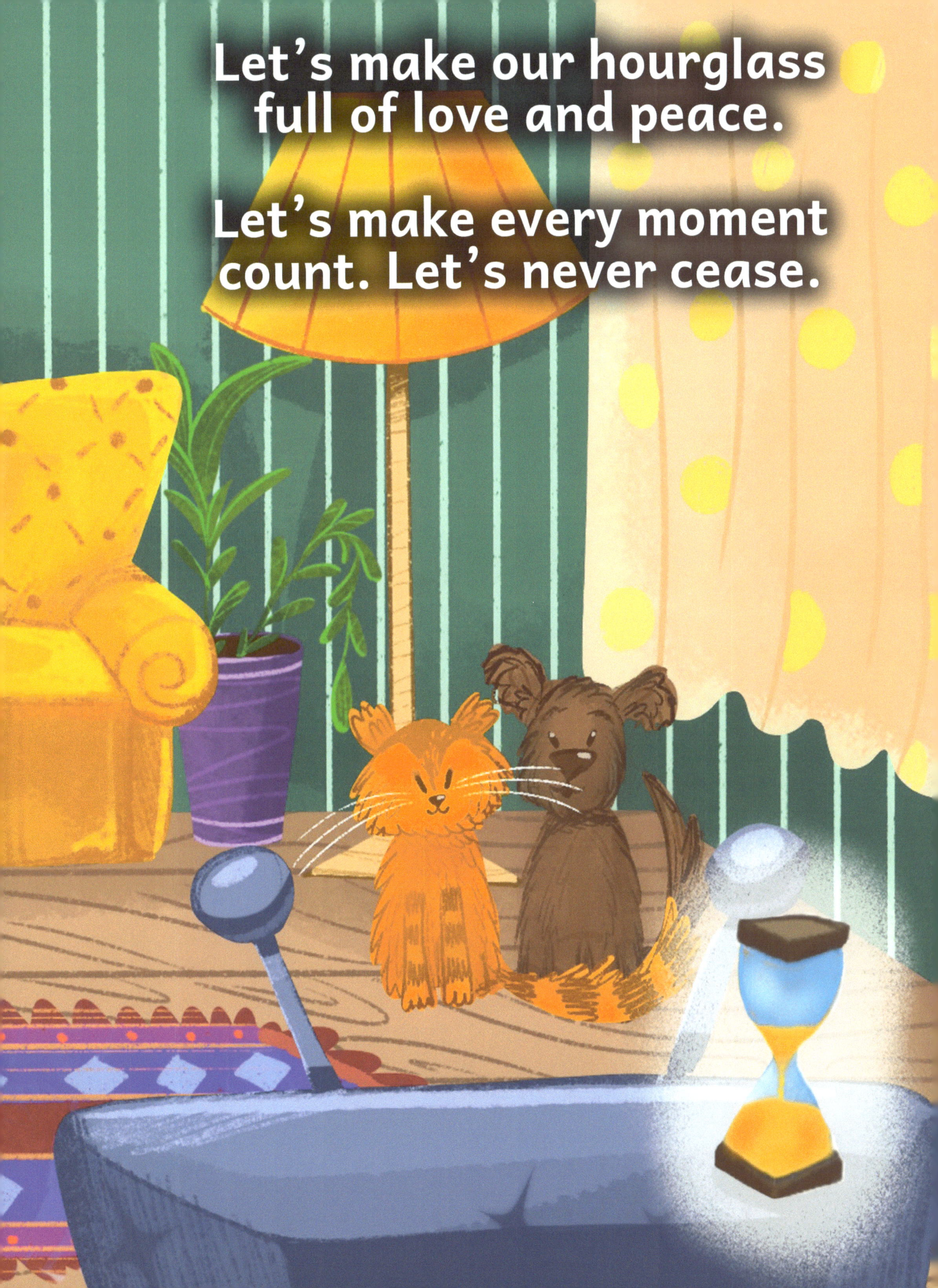

Let's make our hourglass full of love and peace.

Let's make every moment count. Let's never cease.

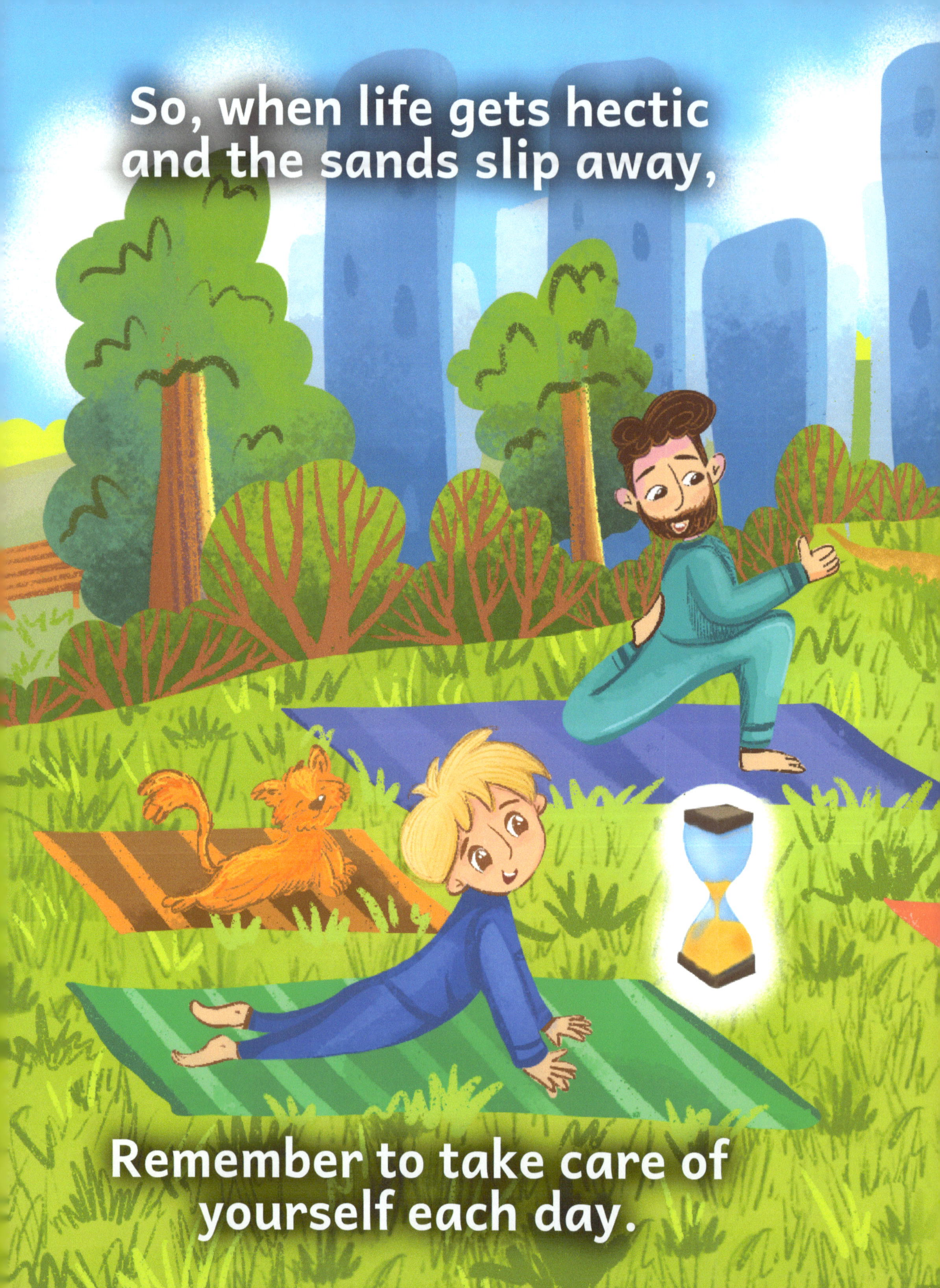
So, when life gets hectic
and the sands slip away,
Remember to take care of
yourself each day.

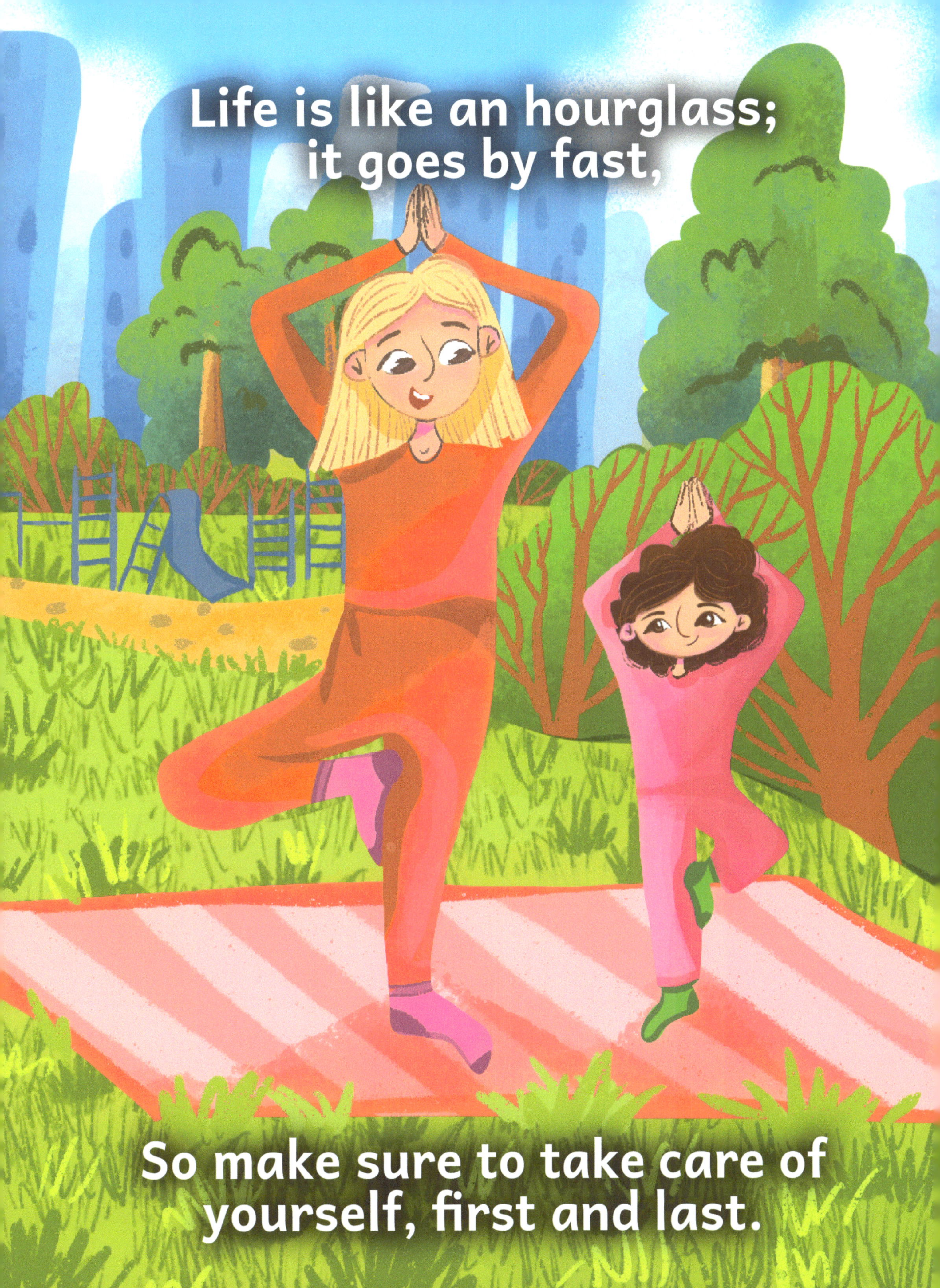
Life is like an hourglass;
it goes by fast,
So make sure to take care of
yourself, first and last.

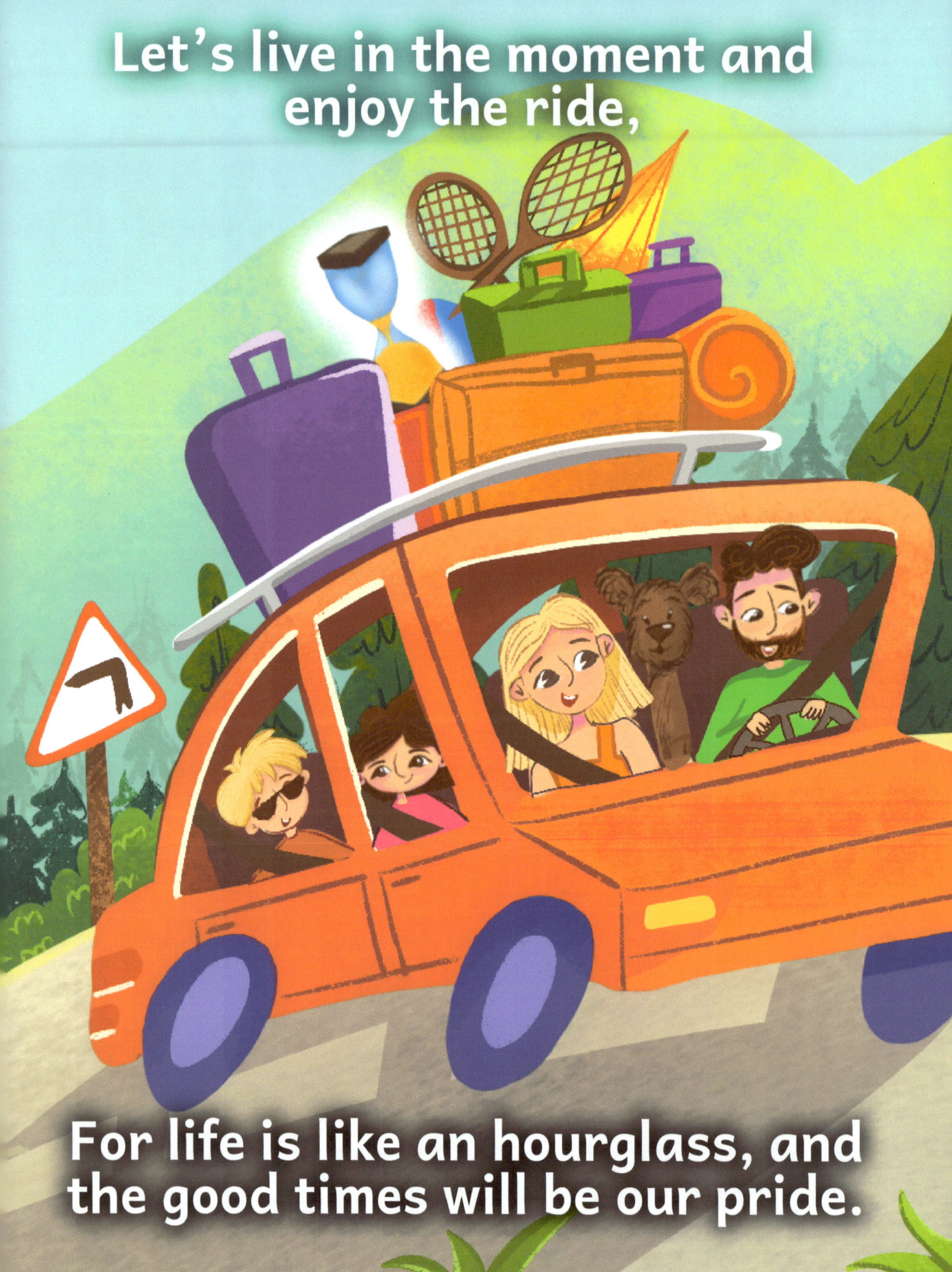

Let's live in the moment and enjoy the ride,

For life is like an hourglass, and the good times will be our pride.

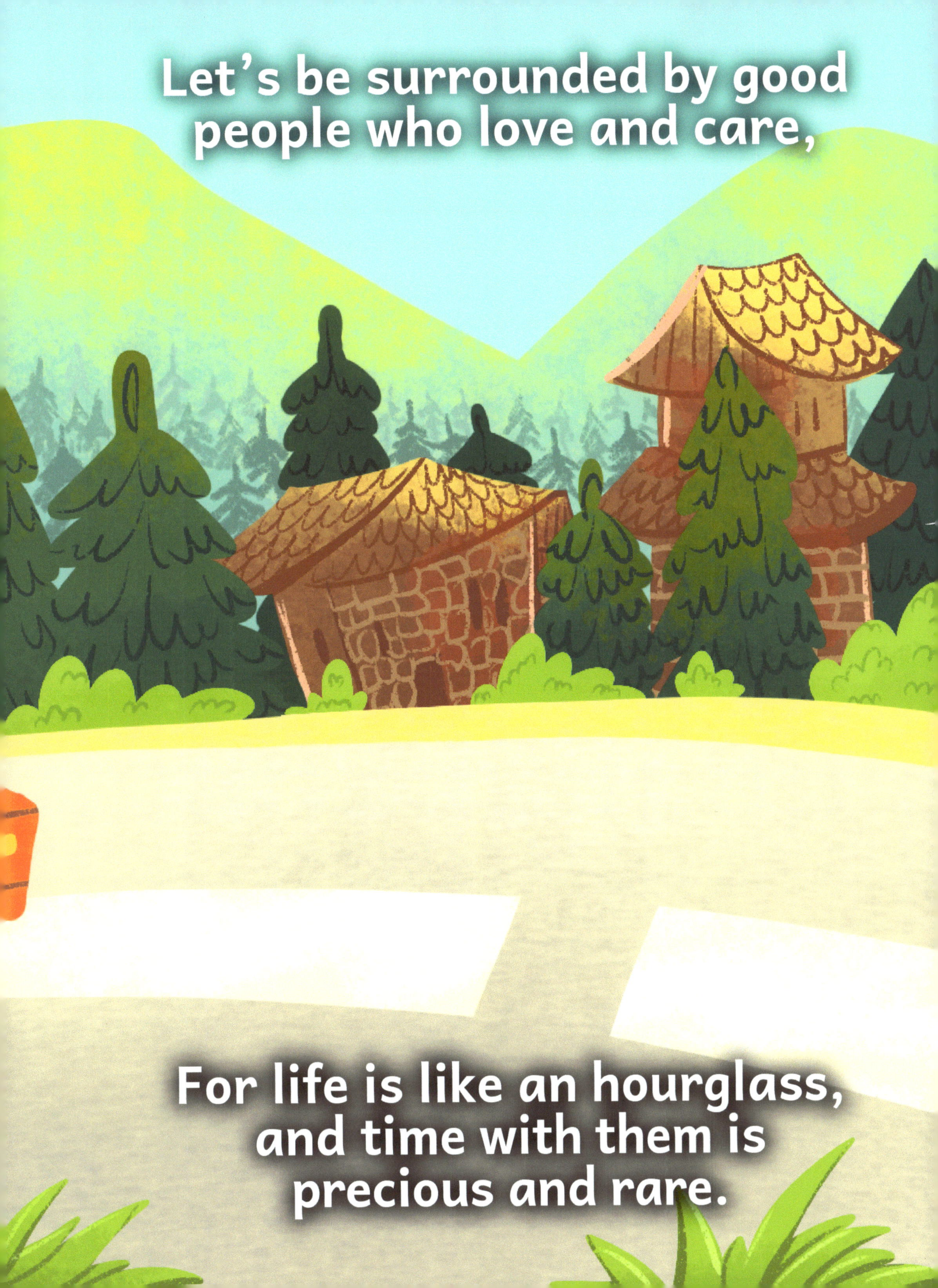

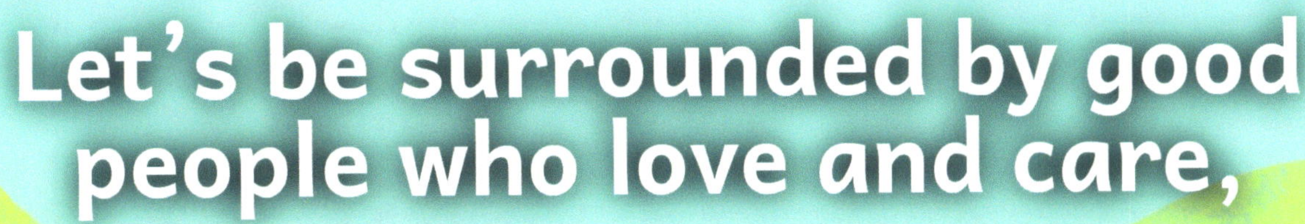

Let's be surrounded by good people who love and care,

For life is like an hourglass, and time with them is precious and rare.

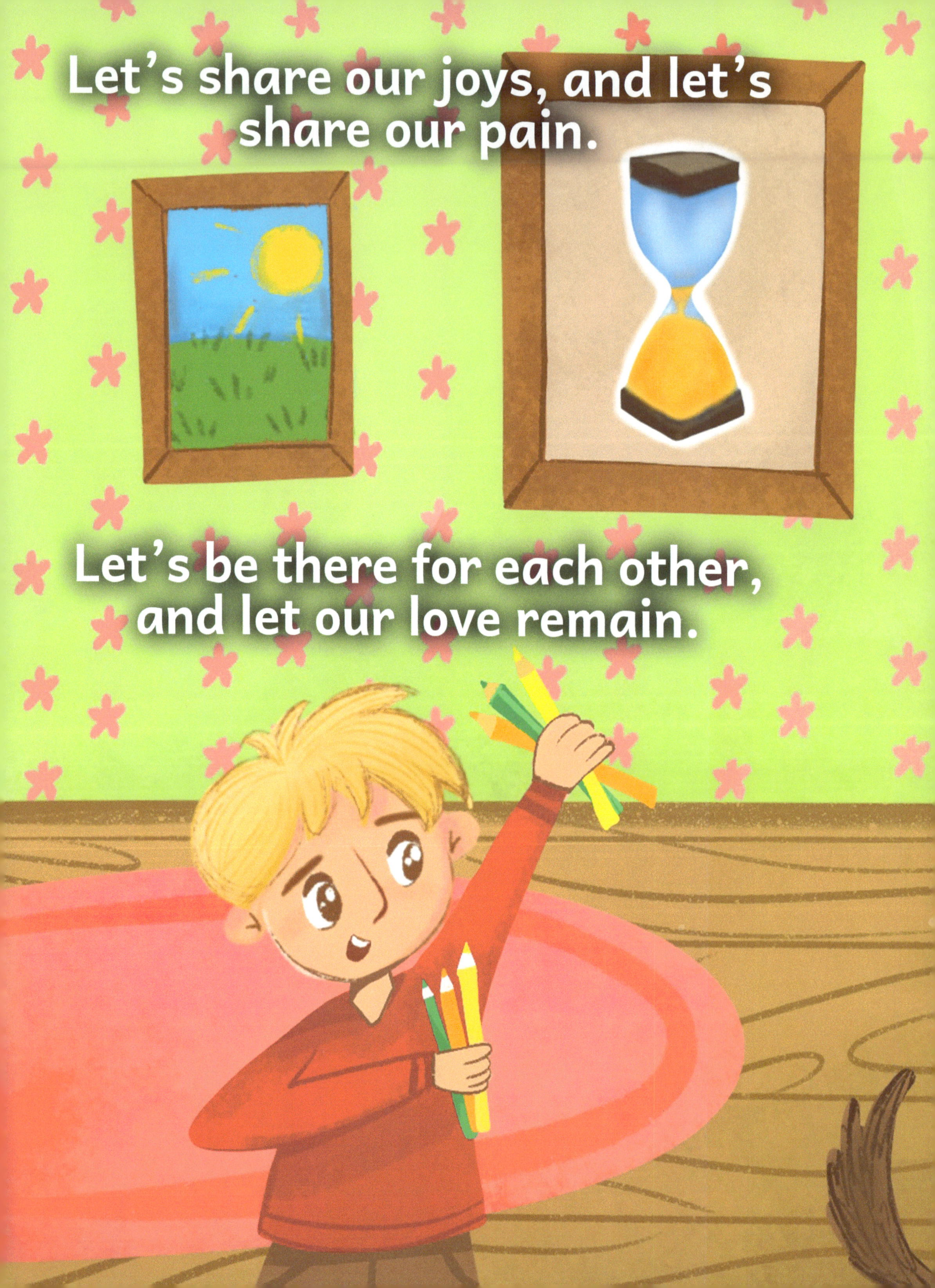
Let’s share our joys, and let’s share our pain.
Let’s be there for each other, and let our love remain.

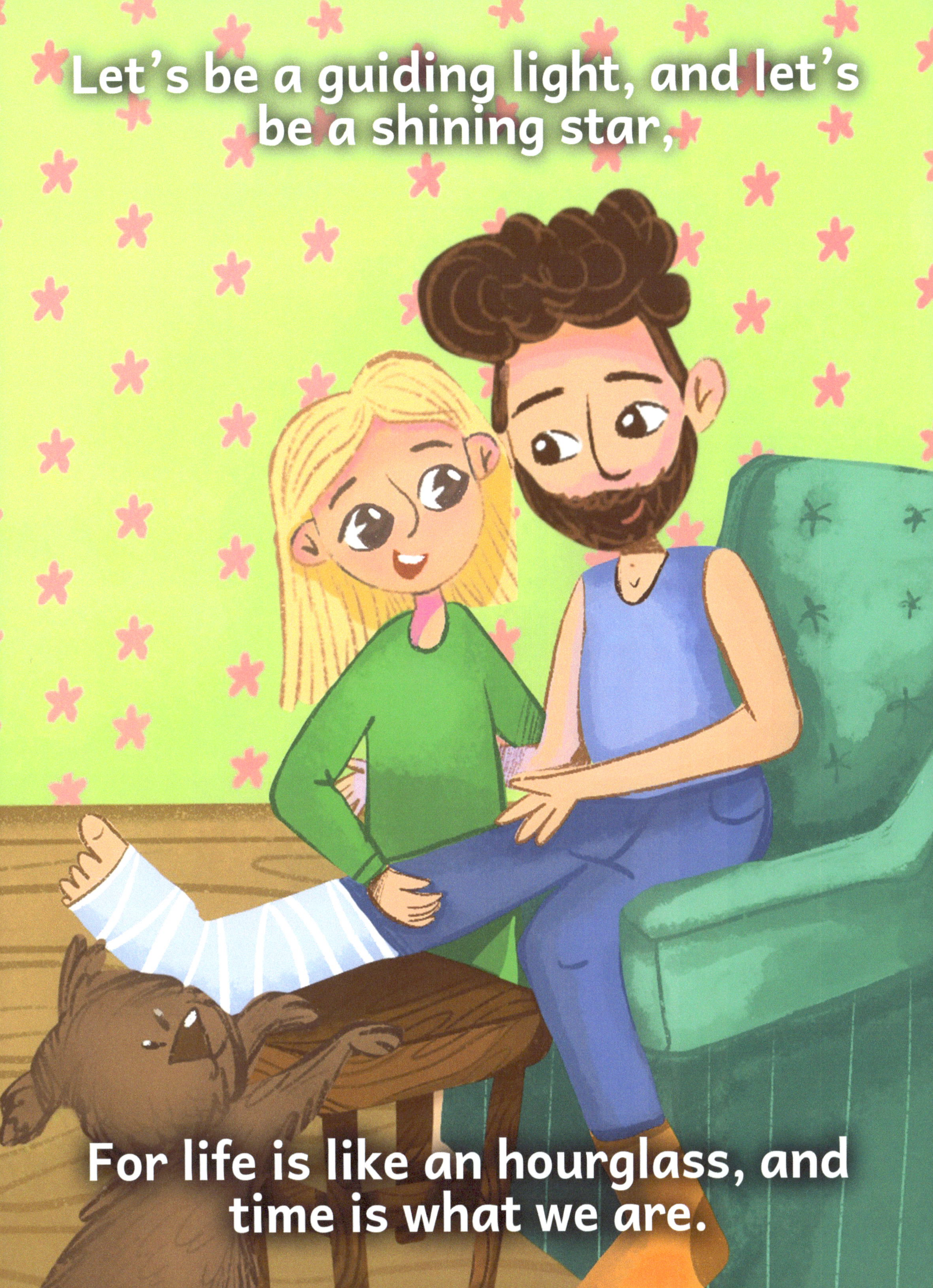
Let's be a guiding light, and let's be a shining star,
For life is like an hourglass, and time is what we are.

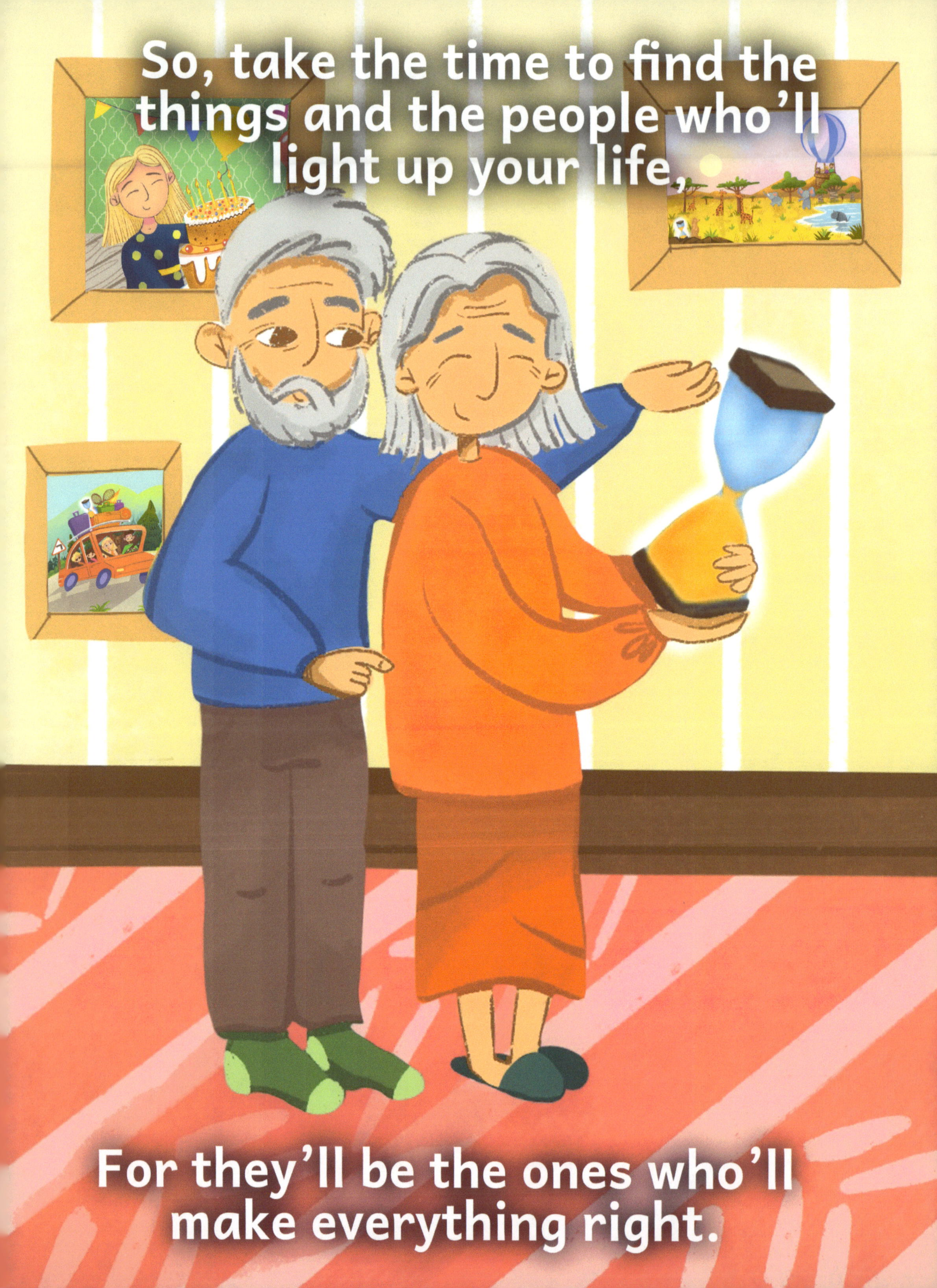

So, take the time to find the things and the people who'll light up your life,

For they'll be the ones who'll make everything right.

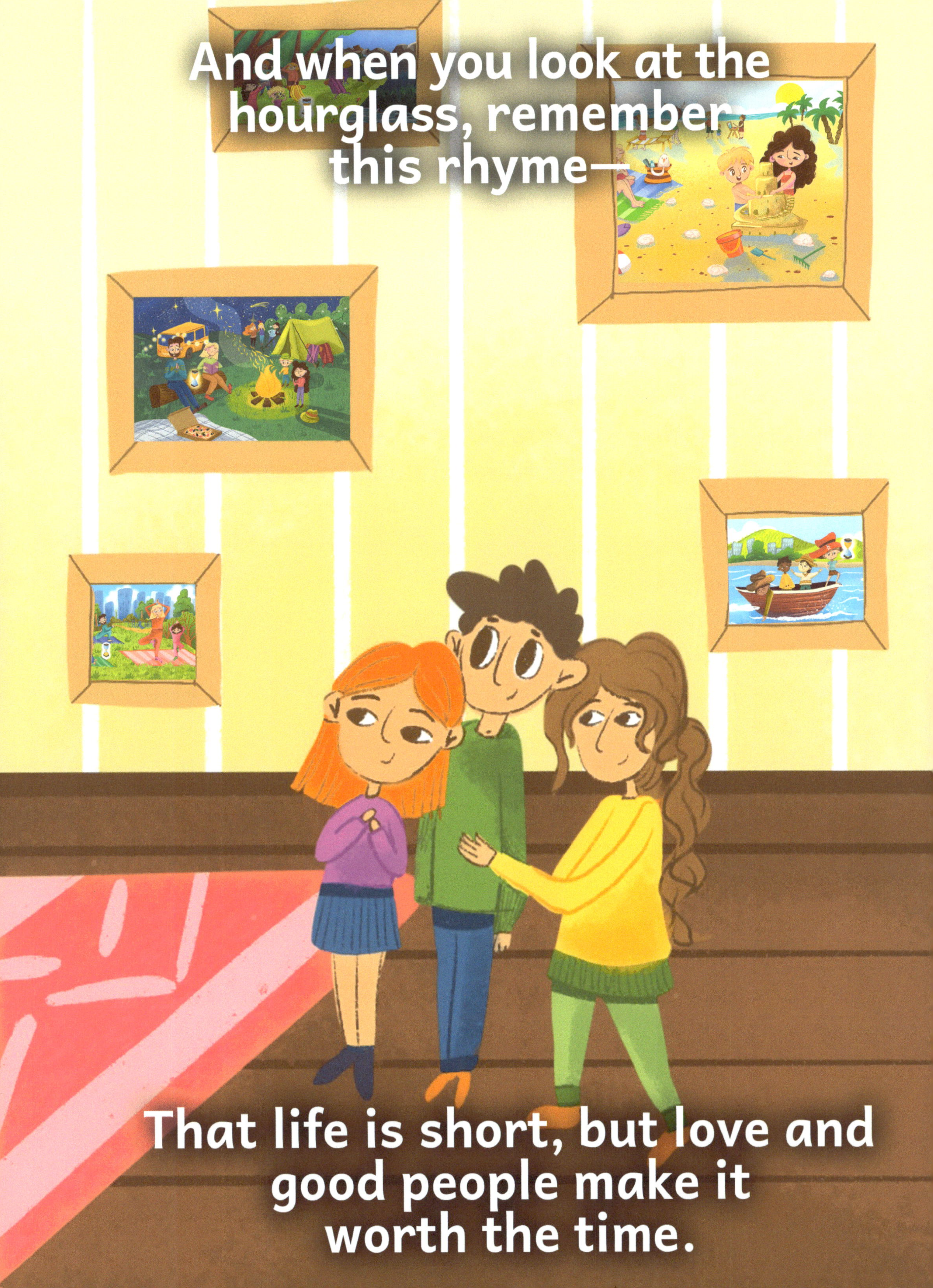
And when you look at the hourglass, remember this rhyme—
That life is short, but love and good people make it worth the time.

Life is like an hourglass because time is constantly passing by, and once it runs out, it's gone. Our time is limited, so we need to make the most of it. We can introduce this analogy to our kids in these ways.

Note for parents/caregivers/guardians—Read and explain this list of tips to your children, since it's far too advanced for them to understand right now.

1. TIME IS LIMITED:

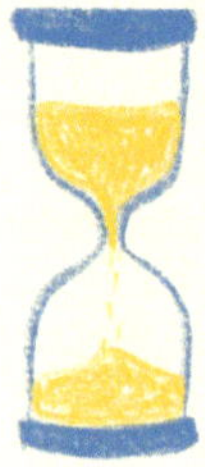

Just like sand in an hourglass, our time here on earth is limited. We have a finite amount of time to spend with our loved ones and should make the most of it.

2. TIME IS PRECIOUS:

Life's precious moments are represented by the sand in an hourglass. Because time is one of our most valuable assets, we should cherish every moment with our loved ones.

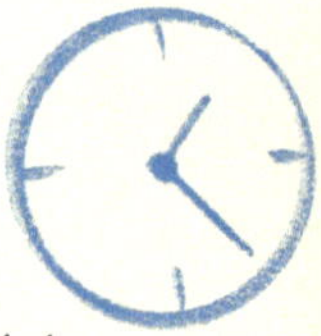

3. MEMORIES ARE IMPORTANT:

Creating cherished memories with our loved ones helps us hold on to them forever. Our memories can help us to stay connected to our loved ones even after they're gone.

4. RELATIONSHIPS MATTER:

Relationships matter a lot in life. Life is about cherishing every moment with the people we love.

5. LOVE IS ESSENTIAL:

The love we have for our loved ones is an essential part of life. It brings us joy, happiness, and fulfillment, and we should never take it for granted.

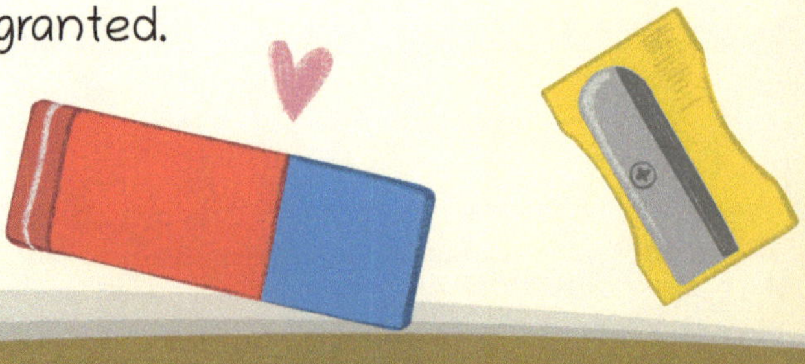

6. LIFE IS A JOURNEY:

You can think of life as an hourglass because it's a journey. We should treasure every moment with our loved ones.

7. FAMILY IS IMPORTANT:

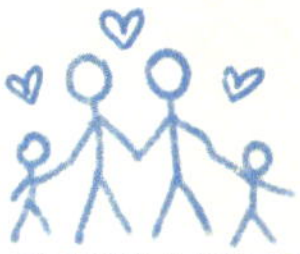

There's nothing like family, and we should cherish every moment we have with them. Through thick and thin, they'll always be there for us.

8. EVERY MOMENT COUNTS:

Life is like an hourglass; every second counts. Make the most of every moment with your loved ones, because you never know when it's the last. Making memories and cherishing every moment helps us make the most of our time.

9. LIFE IS ABOUT EXPERIENCES:

Life is like an hourglass because it's all about the experiences we have. Those we love are the ones who make some of our most memorable moments.

10. MEMORIES LAST FOREVER:

Our memories are some of the most precious things we've got, so cherish them and appreciate them to make them last.

- Life is like an hourglass because experiences make it worth living. Some of our best memories come from the people we love.
- Every moment with our loved ones is important because it helps us create those memories. We shouldn't just think about the big moments, but also the small ones.
- Life's a journey, so we should cherish every moment with our loved ones along the way. Life is a gift, and we should appreciate it with gratitude. It's all about love at the end of the day.

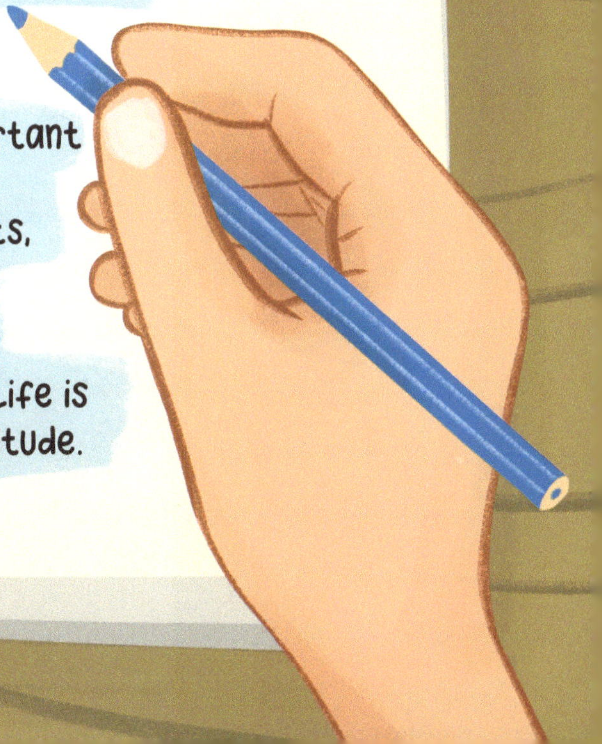

Children can relate to the hourglass analogy by doing these fun activities!

1. Playing with sand timers or hourglasses, and talking about how the sand represents time passing by.

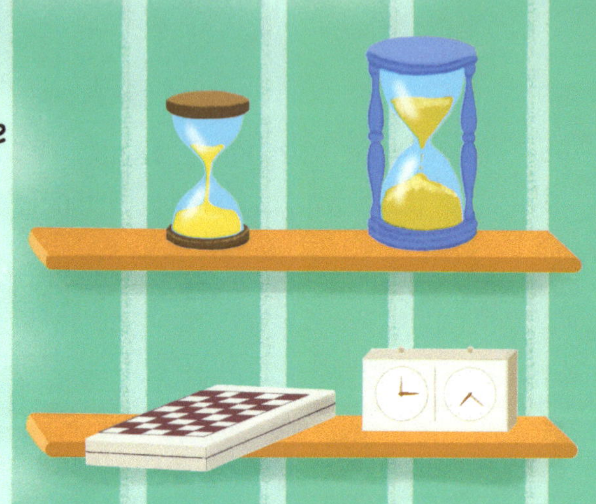

2. Playing a board game with a timer, and discussing how the timer represents the limited time available to complete the game.

3. Making an hourglass craft project, and talking about its symbolism.

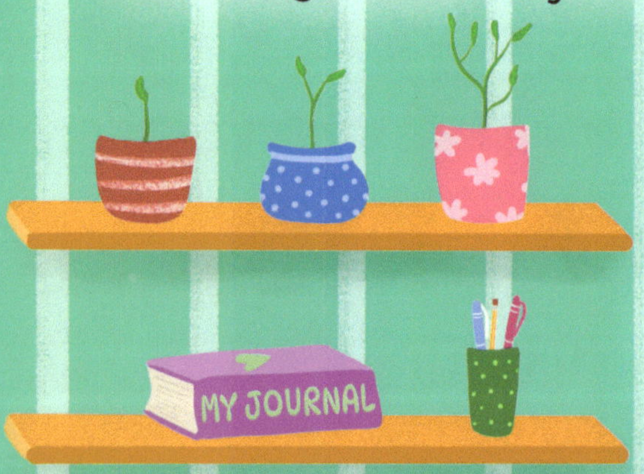

4. Planting seeds and watching them grow, and talking about how things develop over time and how we need to take care of them.

5. Drawing or writing in a journal, and reflecting on how our activities and choices affect our use of time.

6. Going on a nature walk or hike, and talking about how the changing seasons represent the passing of time.

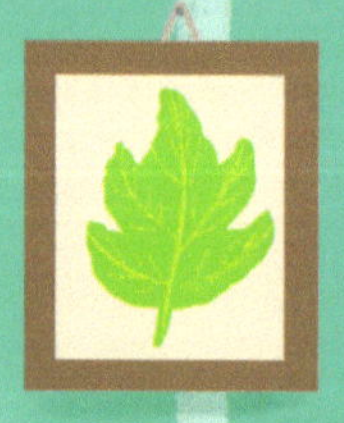
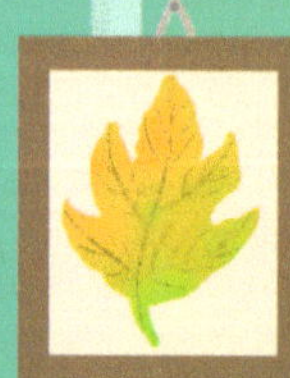
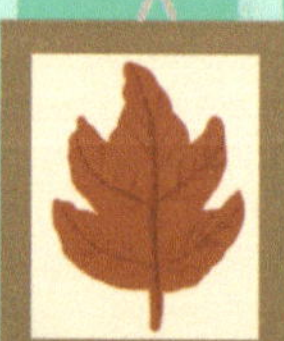

7. Reading a story or listening to a song about time and how we use it, and talking about what we learned.

8. Baking or cooking together, and talking about how time is an important element to any recipe.

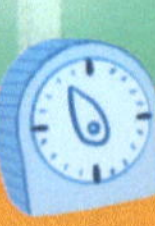

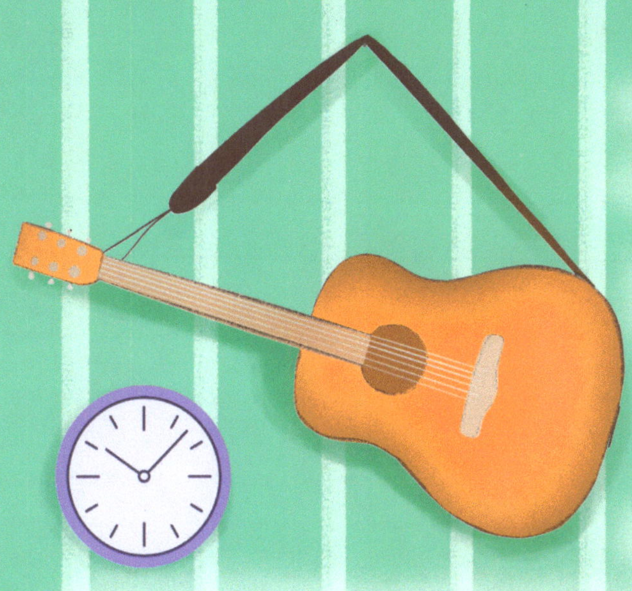

9. Singing or playing an instrument, and discussing how practice and dedication can lead to improvement.

10. Building a time capsule together, and talking about what it means to preserve memories.

11. Exploring a historical site or museum, and learning how the artifacts represent different periods.

12. Making sandcastles on the beach, and talking about how the tide washes them away, reminding us that everything in life is temporary.

13. Taking a road trip or going somewhere new, and talking about how time passes depending on our experiences and what we do with them.

14. Making something beautiful and meaningful by painting or drawing, and talking about how it takes time, patience, and effort.

15. Reading a book together, and talking about how characters' actions and decisions affect their use of time.

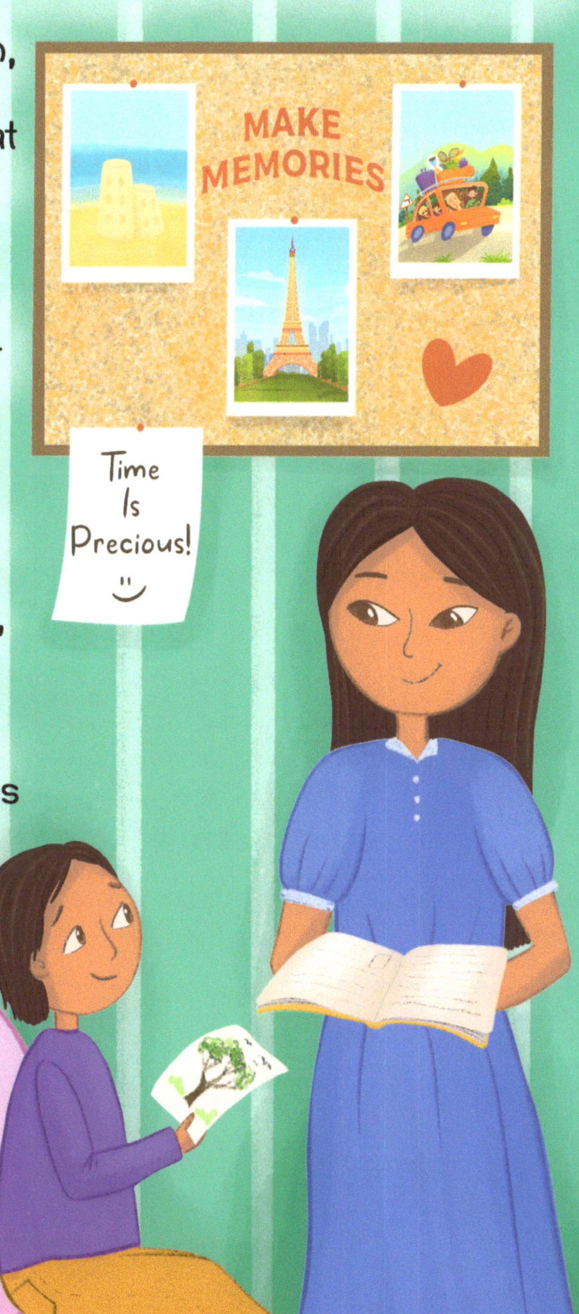

These activities can help kids understand the concept of time as a limited resource and the importance of making the most of it.

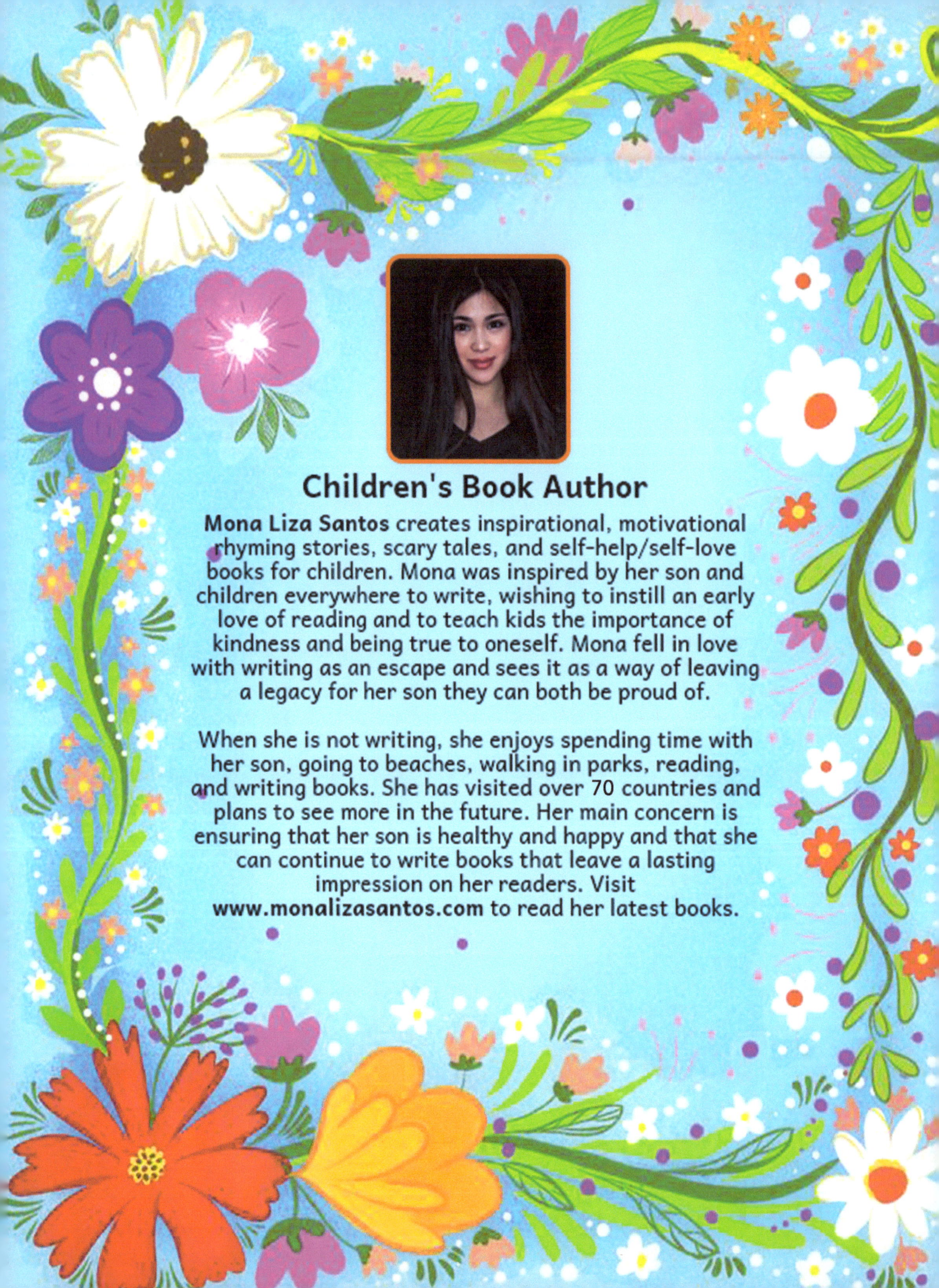

Children's Book Author

Mona Liza Santos creates inspirational, motivational rhyming stories, scary tales, and self-help/self-love books for children. Mona was inspired by her son and children everywhere to write, wishing to instill an early love of reading and to teach kids the importance of kindness and being true to oneself. Mona fell in love with writing as an escape and sees it as a way of leaving a legacy for her son they can both be proud of.

When she is not writing, she enjoys spending time with her son, going to beaches, walking in parks, reading, and writing books. She has visited over 70 countries and plans to see more in the future. Her main concern is ensuring that her son is healthy and happy and that she can continue to write books that leave a lasting impression on her readers. Visit **www.monalizasantos.com** to read her latest books.

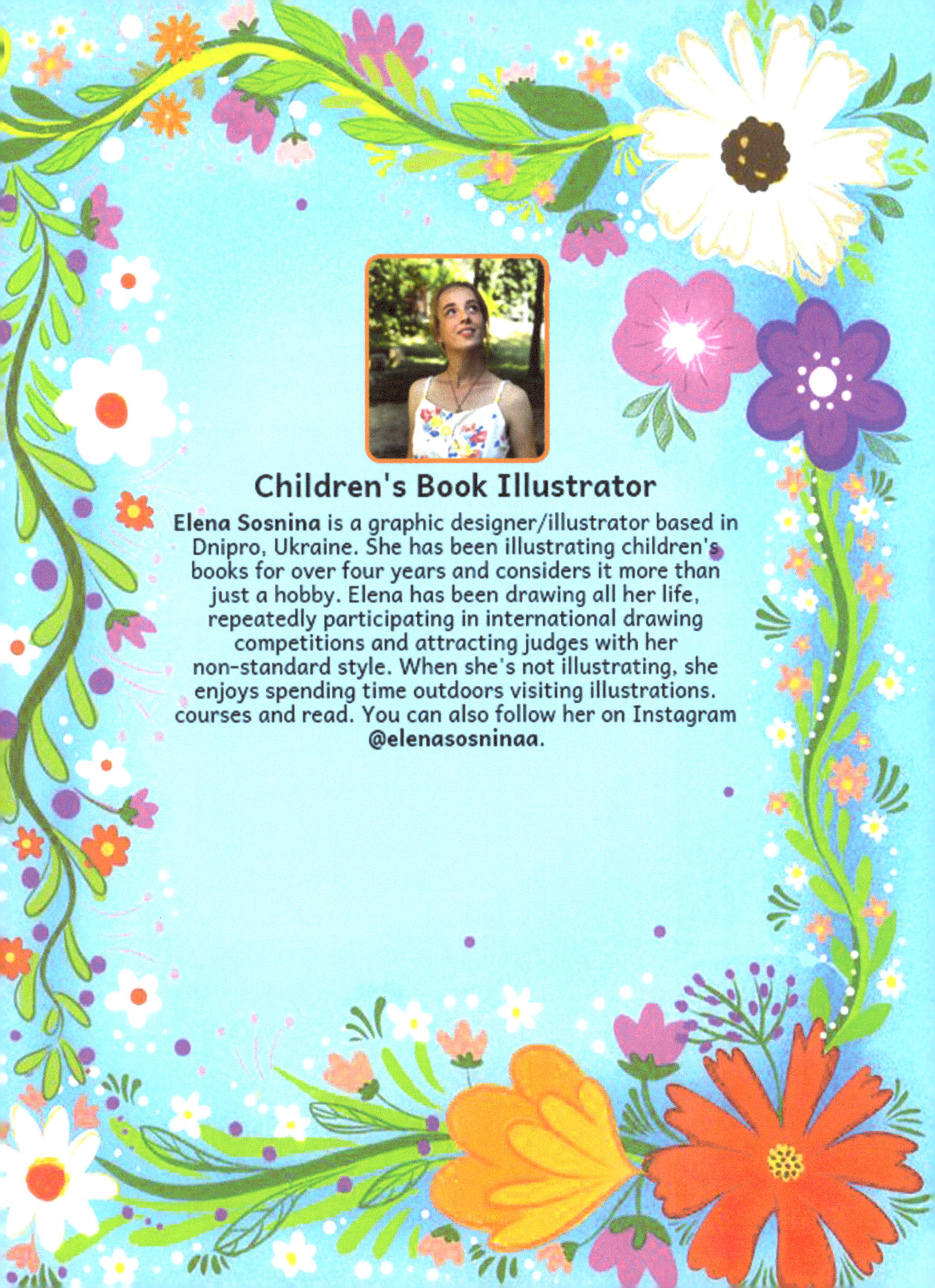

Children's Book Illustrator

Elena Sosnina is a graphic designer/illustrator based in Dnipro, Ukraine. She has been illustrating children's books for over four years and considers it more than just a hobby. Elena has been drawing all her life, repeatedly participating in international drawing competitions and attracting judges with her non-standard style. When she's not illustrating, she enjoys spending time outdoors visiting illustrations. courses and read. You can also follow her on Instagram **@elenasosninaa**.

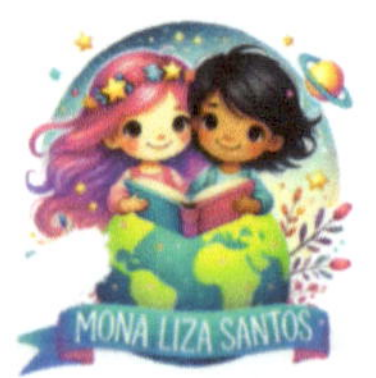

More Books from the Author

By Mona Liza Santos

Discover more stories that inspire kindness, confidence, and imagination. Each book carries a message of courage, compassion, and self-worth—reminding every reader that they are already enough.

💖 Kindness & Empathy

Being Kind Is Cool
No Choosing Favorites
Make Peace, Not War
Let's Be Happy for Each Other
Humble Me
Simon the Jealous Snake
My Mom Is the Whole Village

🌿 Mindfulness & Emotional Resilience

The Hourglass of Life
If I Just Breathe
The Dream Jar
Books Are Life

🌍 Travel & Cultural Exploration

The Many Places We Go
Michael Travels Around the World

🥕 Health Habits & Life Skills

Yummy Veggies
Yummy Fruits
Grown Up Too Soon

🌟 Confidence & Self-Worth

I Am the Chosen One
I Am Brave and Resilient
Surround Yourself
Proud of Me
I Love Me Because I Am Who I Am!
No Choosing Favorites
Let's Be Happy for Each Other
Humble Me
You Are One in a Million
No One Like You

🤝 Friendship & Inclusion

No Choosing Favorites
My Friend Is Different, and That's Okay!

🧚 Fun & Imaginative Adventures

Hmmm... What to Wear
Shadow, My Very Special Unicorn
Blade the Rabbit Learns to Be Grateful
Simon the Jealous Snake

🎄 Seasonal & Holiday Stories

Sam's Magical Christmas

👻 Spooky (But Fun!) Stories

Dark Tales for Kids

Go to Sleep… I Dare You!

❤️ Family & Love

Mama, I Love You

Sam's Magical Christmas

My Mom Is the Whole Village

The Filipino in Me

🐾 Animals & Pets

Oh My Pugs!

Cats Are Love

🔒 Safety

Look Out! Stranger Danger!

🌙 For Older Readers

The Secret Book of Us

I Am Your Karma

The Little Light in the White House

Dark Tales for Kids: 6 Scary Tales for Young Minds

Go to Sleep… I Dare You!

Books Are Life

The Filipino in Me

🌱 Growing Up & Life Lessons

Grown Up Too Soon

You Are One in a Million

🎨 Creativity & Expression

Hmmm… What to Wear

✨ Fantasy, Magic & Wonder

Luna and the Six Evil Witches

Shadow, My Very Special Unicorn

I Am Your Karma

💎 Featured Bestsellers

Mama, I Love You

If I Just Breathe

Proud of Me

I Am the Chosen One

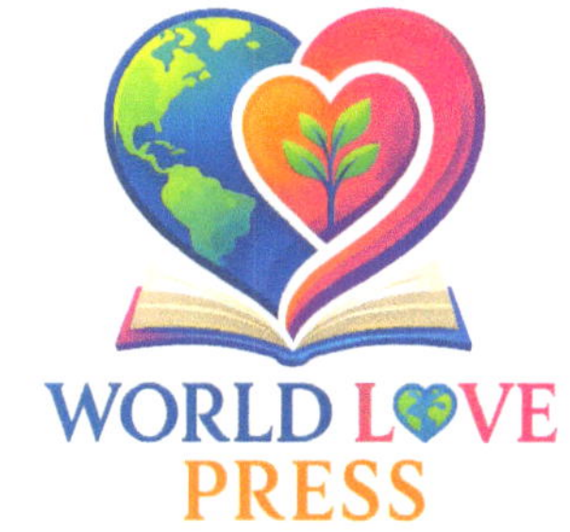

Find all books at:

www.monalizasantos.com

Follow: @momosvoyage

📱 Scan QR to explore the full collection and upcoming releases.

Greetings to my lovely readers!

Please let me start by saying I'm grateful you've read *The Hourglass of Life!* If you could leave me a nice review on Amazon or wherever you got it, it'd mean a lot to me.

I would greatly appreciate your feedback on my book. It would help me brainstorm ideas for future books as well as motivate me to keep writing such inspirational and adorable rhyming poems. In view of the metaphor of life as an hourglass in this book, it is important to remember that it is all about spending it with those you truly care about and making the most of it!

Stay focused on your dreams and stay blessed! Wishing you all a lovely day!

My sincere respect,

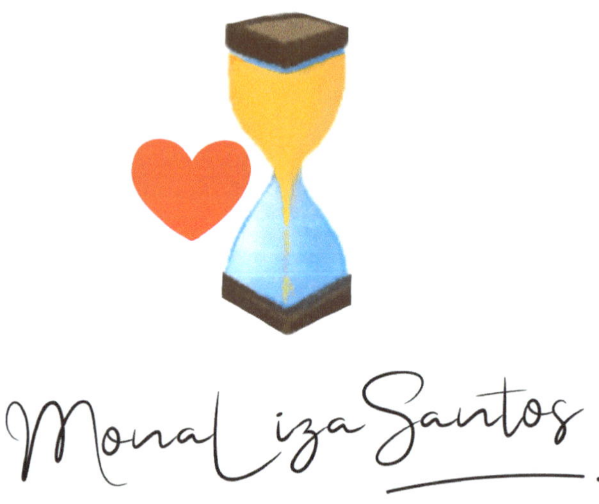

Don't forget to check out my other books on Amazon to see my latest releases and other books you may find inspiring for your young readers as well! Visit my website at www.monalizasantos.com to keep up with me and my books.

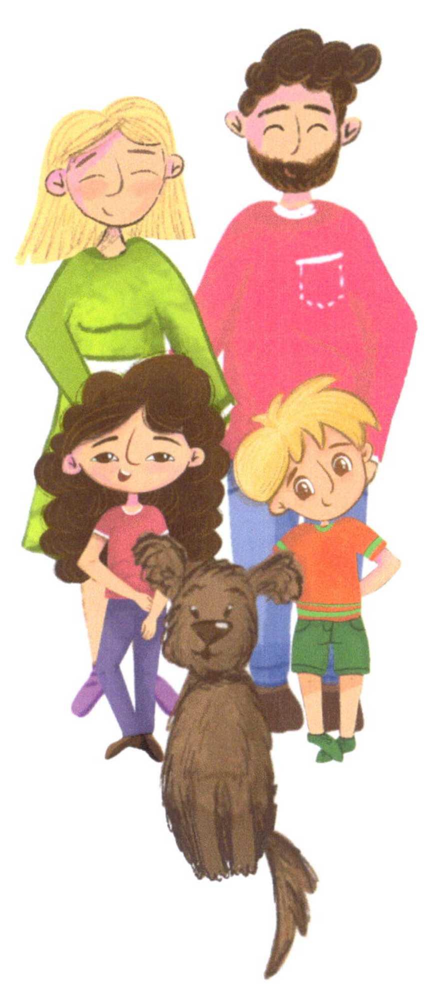

www.ingramcontent.com/pod-product-compliance
Lightning Source LLC
LaVergne TN
LVHW070153110826
845147LV00002B/393
* 9 7 8 1 9 5 5 5 6 0 3 4 4 *